Keyboard Mastery

By
Barbara Grace Ellsworth
Mesa Community College
Mesa, Arizona

Quite often you will use your keyboarding skills to prepare letters, memos, and other business type documents. There are a multitude of word processing programs available and instructions will vary depending upon the word processing program chosen.

Some popular word processing programs you may find:

Microsoft Word
Open Office (from www.OpenOffice.org a FREE full-featured office productivity suite that will even read and save MS Office formats.) We certainly recommend this suite for budget minded users.

Ellsworth Publishing Co. (EPC) offers a free textbook in PDF format that addresses many document formatting concepts. This text is titled *"Nuts and Bolts of Formatting"*, and is available as a free download for current users of EPC products. For our Internet users, this PDF book will be listed at the bottom of the screen showing the licensed products for your school.

Keyboard Mastery

by
Barbara G. Ellsworth
Mesa Community College
Mesa, Arizona

For Information, please contact:

Ellsworth Publishing Company
P.O. Box 6727
Chandler, AZ 85246
www.EllsworthPublishing.com

PRINTED IN THE UNITED STATES OF AMERICA

5-Minute Timing   **S.I.—1.5**

Alexander Fleming was a Scottish bacteriologist on the staff of a hospital in London, England, in 1928. He was studying a germ called Staphylococcus aureus, which caused many ailments from boils to brain disease. In order to study the germs, he grew colonies of them in petri dishes. Each dish held a gelatin food to nourish the germs. One day, Fleming found a spot of green mold in one dish. It was growing on the gelatin among the germs. He realized that a spore from some mold must have settled on the dish while it was uncovered. Fleming did not throw out the spoiled dish because something unusual caught his attention. There was a clear, germ free ring of gelatin around the mold. This meant that the mold had killed the germs there. Fleming watched the mold grow for several days. As the green mold spread, it killed more and more germs. For a long time he gave all his attention to the mysterious mold. It grew and grew. He noticed tiny drops of liquid on the surface of the mold. Perhaps this was the chemical that was destroying the germs. Fleming drew off the liquid, drop by drop. He found that this liquid could kill germs in a test tube. He called the liquid Penicillin.

Fleming published his findings in a British medical journal. Strange as it now seems, the article attracted little attention. Scientists thought it would take too much time and money to produce a useful amount of Penicillin. Apparently Penicillin had been discovered before scientists were ready to develop and use it.

Table of Contents:

5-Minute Timing   S.I.—1.5

The Sumerians wrote on clay. They pressed the end of a
stick into the soft clay, making little three-cornered
marks. They combined these marks to form signs that stood
for words. Since the marks looked like wedges, this form of
writing is called cuneiform, which means wedge-shaped. The
Babylonians, as well as other peoples, borrowed cuneiform
writing from the Sumerians. Clay tablets were heavy and
awkward to handle, but they lasted for centuries. A paper
book buried in the ground for three thousand years would
have rotted away completely. But a clay tablet, carefully
dug up, remains in good condition. Scholars in modern times
have found thousands of the Sumerian and Babylonian tablets
that tell many things about this ancient civilization. They
tell of business and trade in letters from merchants to
their agents. There is a farmer's almanac that gives
instructions about what to plant for each season. A Sumerian
physician wrote down some favorite medical remedies. One of
the most interesting tablets describes what children did in
school four thousand years ago. They hurried to school
because their teacher would beat them with a cane if they
were late. The teacher also used the cane to punish children
for talking, leaving the school without permission, and not
doing lessons properly.

People living together in cities must have laws. The
Sumerians and Babylonians also wrote their laws on tablets
of clay, and sometimes stone. One law provided that people
would have to pay a certain amount of silver if they entered
an orchard that was not their own and were caught stealing.

5-Minute Timing   **S.I.—1.6**

Alcoholism is a disease in which the drinking of alcoholic beverages interferes with the proper functioning of a person's life. The compulsive drinkers drink because they must, in spite of knowing that drinking is affecting their lives in an often disastrous way. It has been said that one-fourth of all social drinkers will end up with severe drinking problems. Alcoholics often show a great change in personality. They may become angry and argumentative, or quiet and depressed. Often a small amount of alcohol causes persons with alcoholism to feel even more anxious, sad, tense, and confused. They then seek relief by drinking more. This is how the alcoholic gets caught up in a web of need and dependency upon alcohol. Many medical problems affect alcoholics. Serious damage to the liver, heart, stomach, and other organs can result from the overuse of alcohol. Many alcoholics do not eat properly, and become ill from poor nutrition. The most tragic effect of alcohol is the damage it causes to the brain. Patients find it difficult to concentrate, their memories are affected, and a few suffer even more serious brain damage. These symptoms and affects are most often permanent and can cause death.

There are programs, such as Alcoholics Anonymous and Al-Anon, which help people overcome the need for alcohol. Many must spend countless hours in meetings to help them stay sober. Alcoholism is a totally preventable disease. One who drinks milk, apple juice, pop, ice tea, water, lemonade, orange juice, grape juice, or any other non-alcoholic drink will never have to worry about it.

★ **Cutting Edge Web-based keyboarding features:**
  - Courses for elementary, middle school, high school, and college.
  - No software to install, update, maintain. All your school needs to maintain is an Internet connection. Upgrades are completed by EPC and available immediately.
  - Courses are self paced; students can work from anywhere (e.g. classroom, home, library, etc).
  - NO PAPERS TO GRADE, HANDLE, PRINT, OR TURN IN TO INSTRUCTOR due to an outstanding teacher management system.
  - Mid-Term and Final Grades are automatically calculated.
  - Monitor and manage all student data online. View scores and grades from the Internet.
  - Special unique software feature prevents students from taking their eyes off the textbook. Solves the age-old problem of students watching their hands or the screen.
  - Use Schedule Manager to select start/end dates, and days/times that students are allowed to work. (Example: If a student is found to be having a friend outside of class do some of his/her work, you can schedule that student's data file only to open during class time).
  - Internal Messaging system to send messages of encouragement/praise to students and receive student replies.
  - Software can be individualized to advanced or special needs students if desired.
  - Create your own custom lessons (create your own 'course within a course').
  - *Nuts 'n' Bolts of Formatting* downloadable textbook free to users of EPC courses—covering Basic Word Concepts, Fax Applications, Interoffice Memos, Business Letters, Proofreader's Marks, Tables, Business Reports, Creating Flyers, Itineraries, Agendas-Minutes-News Releases, Outlines, and Job Search Skills. Directions are on the left and pictures and illustrations on the right—very visual. *We keep up with the latest software versions; schools don't have to purchase thick textbooks that include formatting which become obsolete with each software update.*
  - *Introduction to Microsoft Applications is* downloadable textbook free to users of EPC courses (latest versions)—covering Publisher, Excel, Access, and PowerPoint. Directions are on the left and pictures and illustrations on the right—very visual.
  - Free Site License option to colleges.

★ **There are six essential keyboarding techniques that students should master:**
  - The first day of class students should view the audio/video presentation that illustrates the six essential keyboarding techniques (S. E. C. R. E. T) that are basic to acquiring good keyboarding skills. The keyboarding course demo covers everything necessary for students to begin immediately. Demo's are found on the web site www.KeyboardingOnline.com.

★ **Typists learn speed and accuracy from Lesson 1:**
  - The course standards are created in the Setup by the teacher in the Teacher Manager. Set the Grading Scale for the speed students should achieve by the end of the semester/term. Practice each timing, from Lesson 1, until that speed is reached. If the timing meets the accuracy rate in the Setup, it will record to the Progress Report, from which grades are calculated. Lesson 1 is very easy to assist students in achieving the speed/accuracy goals. This is Competency Based Instruction—master each practice timing until the speed/accuracy goal is achieved before continuing to the next practice timing. All lessons begin with 15– and 30-second timings to encourage the fingers to move quickly.

5-Minute Timing   S.I.—1.5

Benedict Arnold was born in the mid seventeenth century in Norwich, Connecticut. At the age of fourteen, he ran away from his home to fight in the French and Indian War. When the Revolutionary War began, Arnold was already an experienced soldier. He had proven himself to be a heroic soldier and was promoted to the rank of Brigadier General. He fought bravely against the British force on Lake Champlain.

Arnold was placed in command in Philadelphia in 1778. There he married Peggy Shippen, the daughter of a wealthy Loyalist. Life in Philadelphia was very costly and soon he was deeply in debt. Arnold had begun giving important military information to British general Sir Henry Clinton. He did this in anger because he felt that the Continental Congress had not given him the promotions he deserved, and he was desperate for money. He was later given command of West Point. Up to his old tricks, he soon entered into a plot to surrender his strategic post to the British. In return, Arnold was to be made Brigadier General in the British Army and was promised money. British Major John Andre met with Arnold. As Andre was going to New York on horseback, some American soldiers stopped and searched him. They found incriminating papers hidden in his stocking. When Arnold learned that Andre had been seized, he fled to a British ship. The British gave Arnold command of a small British force. He fought against Americans in Virginia and Connecticut. He and his wife and children lived in England where he died there an unhappy man, distrusted by the British as well as by the Americans.

Important Information About The Course, continued:

★ **Experienced typists can improve 10-20 wpm faster than the current speed:**
  - Experienced typists can take the 3-minute *Course Entry* timing, raise the grading scale by 10-20 wpm, and practice each timing until the new goal is reached.

★ **Block the timing screen to encourage students to keep their eyes on the copy, not their fingers or the keys:**
  - Fast and productive typists can type without looking at their keys.
  - The timing screen can be blocked so students cannot see what they have typed until after the practice timing. If they look away from the copy to their fingers or keys, they will usually lose their place and make an error. All lessons begin with 15-second timings and usually 0 errors (set by instructor). If the errors allowed are exceeded the timing score will not record. Students learn from the beginning to keep their eyes on the copy, which helps them learn the keys faster.

★ **Alphabetic keys are reviewed four times:**
  - Section A in the textbook contains information necessary to enable students to get started quickly and progress independently on their own. It should be read by teachers and students. Sections B, C, D, and E review all keyboard letters.
    - Section B is designed to achieve speed and accuracy while learning the keys A-Z.
    - Section C reviews the letters A-Z again with special timings that emphasize each letter.
    - Section D contains short timings to teach numbers and symbols, and longer timings to increase keyboarding skill.
    - Section E contains ten additional timings of longer duration (3-5 minutes). The first and second optional timing are used for the *Course Entry* and *Course Exit* timing.

★ **Create your own custom lessons:**
  - Instructors can create their own timed and graded lessons. These created lessons become part of the student's progress report and grade (created lessons are treated just like any other lesson in the course).
  - This allows instructors to create their own 'course within a course'. Do students need extra practice with medical terminologies, longer timings, etc.? Create your own lessons to fit your own needs!

Time Requirements:
Lessons   1-11 = Approximately 25 hours
Lessons 12-24 = Approximately 15 hours
Lessons 25-33 = Approximately 15 hours
Optional Timings = Varies based upon number of assignments

Supporting Materials:
No additional materials are necessary for either the teacher or student—the courses are self-contained with the textbook and software only.

5-Minute Timing   S.I.—1.5

What does the word intelligence mean? Are animals intelligent? Animals cannot speak or learn history, but they can do other things. The cat can be taught to ring the doorbell when it wants to come in the house. Circuses are filled with dancing bears, playful sea lions, prancing horses, and elephants that can do tricks. Such behavior is often incorrectly interpreted as signs of intelligence. The ability to reason is the essence of intelligence. It is the sudden flash of an idea. It is the ability to solve a new problem by utilizing previous experience. Performing tricks and tasks do not require the ability to reason, to think, to have new ideas.

Tricks and tasks can be mastered through special kinds of learning. There is trial and error, and conditioned responses. For example, if a bell is rung every time an animal is fed, the animal soon learns to look for food when it hears the bell. Animals can learn to avoid a place or an object by being given a mild, harmless electric shock. Some can even be forced to change their normal behavior. For example, cockroaches usually come out only in the dark. They hide in dark places during the daytime. In one experiment, some cockroaches were placed in a box. One half was lighted and the other half dark. As was expected, the cockroaches scurried into the dark half. Once inside the dark half, they were given a shock that they didn't like. After a number of electric shocks, they kept away from the dark and stayed in the light. This was against their nature; however, they disliked the electric shocks even more than they disliked the light.

About the Author:

Barbara G. Ellsworth has taught at Mesa Community College for 45+ years. For many years Mrs. Ellsworth taught Business Machines (she says she started teaching when she was 12). During that time she wrote and published over 42 workbooks for various Ten-Key and calculating machines. Mrs. Ellsworth currently has written and published five web-based courses—*Ten Key Mastery, Keyboard Mastery, Keyboard Short Course, Skillbuilding Mastery, Keyboarding For Kids (Grades 1-6), Nuts 'n' Bolts Formatting, and Introduction to MS Applications.* Her products are found at all educational levels—K-12, College/Adult, job corps., as well as in government institutions and commercial businesses.

Tutorials, demonstrations, course descriptions, downloads, current syllabi, and online course information can be seen at:

www.EllsworthPublishing.com

Course Descriptions

★ **TEN KEY MASTERY** — (Approximately 30 hours) To teach the numeric keypad with speed and accuracy. Course includes three actual employment tests for students to practice. To achieve employment standards, it is recommended to be a quarter or semester course.

★ **KEYBOARD MASTERY** — (Approximately 60 hours) To teach the alpha/numeric keyboard to beginners and to those who haven't typed in a long time and have rusty skills. The course contains 15-second to 5-minute timings that cover the basics. This course can be customized for either a semester or a quarter course.

★ **KEYBOARD SHORT COURSE** — (Approximately 25 hours) A shortened version of KEYBOARD MASTERY. It covers the alphabetic and punctuation keys (no numeric or symbol keys). It is designed for approximately 5 - 9 weeks. The course contains mainly 15-second timings which push for speed and accuracy, and includes 30-second, 1- and 2-minute timings. This course is excellent for beginners and experienced typists who need to raise their skills quickly.

★ **SKILLBUILDING MASTERY** — (Approximately 60 hours) Advanced Keyboarding. Covers alpha and numeric/symbol keys with 15-second to 5-minute timings designed to bring students to employable levels of speed and accuracy. It is recommended that students type approximately 32-35 wpm before taking this course.

★ **KEYBOARDING FOR KIDS** — (Approximately 20-40 hours) For Grades 1 - 6. Teaches keyboarding correctly to children at a time when they are exposed to computers, and to prevent the formation of bad keyboarding habits. The short timings and textbook help keep student's eyes away from the screen and fingers. Students are rewarded with graphics of praise when they meet their goal.

★ **NUTS 'n' BOLTS FORMATTING** — A FREE download (PDF book) for current EPC users covering basic document processing—letters, tables, faxes, memos, business reports, etc.

★ **INTRODUCTION TO MICROSOFT APPLICATIONS** — A FREE download (PDF book) for current EPC users covering: Publisher, Excel, Access, and PowerPoint.

Keyboard Mastery • Introduction   © 1992-2015 Ellsworth Publishing Co.   vii
www.EllsworthPublishing.com

5-Minute Timing S.I.—1.4

For years people have watched snake charmers in Indian bazaars play music to their cobras. The watchers have marveled at the way the snakes seem to move in response to the music. But a little research shows that a snake cannot hear sounds that are high pitched. If a cobra is blindfolded, you can play music on a pipe for hours and the snake will sit still. If you remove the blindfold and wave your arms around, the snake will raise its head and spread its hood. A cobra responds not to the music, but to the movements the snake charmer makes as he plays.

It is difficult to enter the world of animals. Too often we think of animals as if they were human beings. It is hard to realize that they do not see as we see, smell as we smell, or hear as we hear. Yet anyone who does not realize this is bound to make mistakes. Many experiments can be done in the field, outside of the laboratory. If you change some factor in the life of a group of animals, how will the animals respond? And how does this behavior compare with the behavior of the control group kept in normal surroundings? Scientists have to be very careful to make sure that the animals are reacting only to the sights and sounds provided in the experiment and not to something else. Even the experimenter can ruin an experiment. One scientist was studying how geese responded to a cardboard model of an enemy. The enemy was a bird of prey flying overhead. Before each test, the experimenter had to climb a tree to fasten the model overhead. Very soon the geese were giving an alarm call every time the experimenter started to climb the tree.

Why should I learn keyboarding?

The most simple answer is a one word answer: **Productivity**.

The future workforce you will be a part of, and compete with, is increasingly global. This means that you will be competing with other persons not in your city, or even in your state. Companies and their workforce must compete with workers in other countries willing to do the same job, and often times for less money. How do U.S. companies compete against lower wage countries and a workforce eager for employment? Getting more work done with fewer hours worked = Productivity.

In the 21st century, a common theme of distress is the outsourcing of jobs outside of the U.S. Consider the following statement from the May 2004 issue of Business 2.0 (full PDF of article available at: www.EllsworthPublishing.com/Articles/Keyboarding_And_Outsourcing.pdf)

"For American service workers to hang on to their jobs, they will have to make similar changes. Barry P. Bosworth, a senior fellow in economic studies at the Brookings Institution, points out that the fastest-growing service fields are the engineering and management of computerized sales and supply systems. To shine in those careers, he says, **workers have to master at least four skills: computer literacy, <u>typing</u>, an understanding of how complex organizations work, and the ability to deal with people (either in person or electronically). Yet despite the fact that services account for 80 percent of private-sector employment, how many high schools require courses in <u>typing</u>, computer science, operations research, and interpersonal relations?** *Talk about productivity: If critics want to be truly effective at keeping jobs at home, they should stop scolding businesses and start crusading for better education reform."*

<u>But Voice Recognition software is going to replace the keyboard, right</u>? For debate, we will look at the best case scenario for Voice/Speech recognition software and we will assume that recognition software has matured into the perfect product and has overcome the following hurdles:

(1) No problems recognizing accents, slurred speech, speech when you are sick, speech from different parts of the country, or sounds that people sometimes misarticulate (just ask a Speech-Language pathologist).
(2) It needs no training, it instantly recognizes the speech characteristics of any person that sits down at any given computer.
(3) The software is found everywhere and on every computer.
(4) The software has mastered short-cuts and enhancements that make speaking faster in all ways rather than typing/keyboarding (think web browsing and data entry).

Assuming that recognition software is perfect, there are many social and economic issues that will always necessitate keyboarding skills. If you can answer 'Yes' to the following situations, then the keyboard will become obsolete, otherwise, better plan on keeping it as part of your curriculum:

(1) In your lab, it would be preferable to have students dictate their term papers/book reports to the computer. The noise would not be a distraction.
(2) During class (K-12 or college classes), it would be best if students could dictate lecture notes into their laptop rather than have to type them.
(3) While attending a conference, you decide to use one of the email stations. You would rather dictate your email alongside everyone else who is dictating their emails (privacy, privacy, privacy).
(4) In an office environment, all secretaries and data-entry employees could dictate memos, reports, etc., without disturbing employees or worrying about confidentiality.
(5) and so on, and so on.

There are social and privacy reasons that can never be overcome with even the best recognition software. There will certainly be uses for voice recognition software, but it will not make the keyboard obsolete.

Keyboard Mastery • Introduction   © 1992-2015 Ellsworth Publishing Co.   viii
www.EllsworthPublishing.com

4-Minute Timing   S.I.—1.3

The holes in a piece of bread are made by bubbles of gas. To make bread, flour and water (and other ingredients) are mixed to form a dough. Then a small amount of yeast is added to the mixture. Yeast is a type of fungus that grows very quickly when it is warm and damp. While the yeast is growing, it gives off a gas that bubbles up through the dough, making it expand. The yeast gives bread a particular flavor and appetizing smell. No one knows when yeast was first used to make bread, but it must have been many thousands of years ago. According to one story, it happened by accident. Some yeast is said to have been placed into the dough by chance and it made it rise. Because this loaf was twice as big as normal, people thought it must be magic. However, the bread tasted better than the usual flat, heavy loaves, so they soon used yeast to make all their bread.

Cakes also have holes in them made by bubbles of gas. But these are made by a baking powder that leaves practically no flavor. Baking Powder is a mixture of tartaric acid and bicarbonate of soda. When these two chemicals are mixed together with moisture and heated, they react to produce carbon dioxide. The carbon dioxide bubbles through the cake mixture to make it rise while it is being baked.

SECTION A

General Information

4-Minute Timing   S.I.—1.5

A famous bronze statue of the little Mermaid, carved by Edvard Eriksen, is poised on a rock in a harbor in Denmark. She is the heroine of a fairy tale by Hans Christian Andersen about a mermaid who falls in love with a prince and who sacrifices her tongue to exchange her fish tail for human legs.

Hans Christian Andersen was born in Denmark. His childhood was one of poverty and neglect. When he was fourteen years old, he went to Copenhagen to try to be an actor or opera singer. Hans became an apprentice at the Royal Theater and attracted influential patrons who provided him with his first real education. He was not very successful in acting and turned to writing. A friend who had faith in his talent persuaded the King of Denmark to grant him a pension so that he could continue his education and travel to other countries. Soon afterwards, he began to write poems, plays, novels, and travel books that sold very well. Today, the accomplishments of Hans Christian Andersen are all but forgotten and the world remembers him mainly for his fairy tales. They are now published in more than eighty languages. Among his famous tales of fantasy are The Ugly Duckling, The Emperor's New Clothes, The Snow Queen, The Red Shoes, and The Little Mermaid.

KNOW YOUR PROGRAM — Watch the course demo at www.KeyboardingOnline.com

1. To become an excellent typist there are <u>six absolutely essential techniques</u>:

   S _ _ **U** _ Straight, a _ _ _ and w _ _ _ _ _ straight.

   E _ _ _ on the b _ _ _ .

   C _ _ _ _ _ _ **F** _ _ _ _ _ _ _ _. Keep your " _ " finger on the " _ " key when depressing the
   Enter key. Keep your fingers near the H _ _ _ R _ _ . Each finger depresses its own keys.

   R _ _ _ _ _ _ _ _ _ **R** _ _ _ _ _ . Keep an even, steady pace. Eliminate pauses.

   E _ _ _ _ _ _ _ _ errors properly, if allowed by your teacher.

   T _ _ _ **K** _ _ _ _ as if they were hot.

2. If your typing area turns grey and cannot see what you have typed your instructor has enabled the
   B_ _ _ _out Timing is enabled.

3. The U _ _ _ I _ _ _ screen is where you can change your password.

4. The S _ _ _ _ contains all of your course standards. Click on the tabs to see the course standards.

5. The E _ _ _ _ _ _ A _ _ _ _ _ _ _ column shows the accuracy needed to have a timing recorded. If
   you have too many errors, take the timing again.

6. When you finish a lesson, a c _ _ _ _ _ m _ _ _ will appear in the box on the left.

7. On single line exercises do not press the S _ _ _ _ _ _ _ at the end of the line, press the E _ _ _ _
   key and keep going until the timer stops. The timer begins when the first key is depressed.

8. If you begin a timing with errors you can start over by clicking on the T _ _ _ _ button.

9. To make letters larger on the screen move the A _ _ _ _ _ F _ _ _ button to the right.

10. The P _ _ _ _ _ _ _ R _ _ _ _ _ shows your best timing scores.

11. The current grade and final grade are based on the B _ _ _ score for each lesson line on the
    Progress Report.

12. The C _ _ _ _ _ _ Grade Report shows your overall average WPM (non-weighted) with a grading
    scale to help you evaluate your progress.

13. The F _ _ _ _ Grade Report shows your final weighted timing grade when A _ _ the assigned
    lessons have been completed.

14. Can you go back to your Progress Report at any time and practice to improve your scores and
    grade? (Yes / No)

15. The M _ _ _ _ _ _ Center can be used to communicate with your instructor.

3-Minute Timing   S.I.—1.5

The sparsely settled interior of Australia is known as the outback. Cattle raising is the chief economic activity. Ranches, called stations, are far apart. The loneliness of life in the outback is rapidly disappearing. Most stations have their own airstrips for use by their own and other planes. Outback children are far from any school. Some children go to boarding schools in the cities, but most listen at home to a program called School of the Air. Assignments are given out over the radio and the children mail in their homework to be graded.

The radio also helps when people become sick. In the early days many sick people died because there were no doctors or hospitals nearby. But today the Royal Flying Doctor Service makes doctors and dentists available throughout the outback. Radio also reduces some of the loneliness of life for people in the outback. It provides most of their entertainment, and people sometimes use it to chat with their neighbors, who are often too far away to visit easily.

Keyboarding Online:

1. Open your Internet browser (i.e. Internet Explorer, Firefox, Chrome, Safari, etc.)
2. Go to: login.KeyboardingOnline.com.
3. The school login and password is given by your instructor (EPC does not provide login instructions to students, this must be provided by your instructor). Your instructor may have qualification or attendance requirements needed before beginning the online class.
4. Click on the icon for your course.
5. (A) Choose your class, (B) Select your name.
6. Enter your ID/Password, this is different from the login/password used to get into login.KeyboardingOnline.com (your instructor will inform you of your ID/Password). You are now into your course.
7. Click the *Setup* in the main menu to see the course standards. Click on *Introduction* and go through all steps. Click *Lessons Menu* to take timings.
8. You will be prompted for an access code when opening any lesson screen. If you do not have an online access code on the easel of this book, you may purchase a code at: store.KeyboardingOnline.com.

A clairvoyant is a person who possesses the power to discern or detect objects without using the usual senses of seeing, hearing, touching, tasting, or smelling. The small number of people with this form of extra-sensory perception can be said to possess a sixth sense. Many people skeptical of clairvoyance and telepathy have been forced to admit that such phenomena cannot be explained in terms of the laws of normal physics and psychology.

A simple method of detecting clairvoyance is to have a person hold a shuffled pack of cards face down. The person is then asked to guess the top card, then the next one, and so on throughout the deck. Usually the pack of cards will be in front of the clairvoyant, but sometimes it is not even in the same room. Experiments at various psychic research centers have produced some remarkable successes. One famous clairvoyant is recorded as having seen a crashed car on a road which, to all other observers, was absolutely deserted. Only a day later a car did crash on the exact spot previously seen.

SETUP—ENTERING COURSE STANDARDS

The *Setup* screen asks for *Name*, *ID#*, *Options*, *Timing Weights*, *Sections*, and *Grading Scale*. These course standards will appear on the *Final Grade Report*. (For the Internet version, the instructor would already have completed the *Setup* for you).

Name: First and last name.

ID#: Roster number/student ID# Students will need to know this number/word in order to open their file (files are password protected).

Options: <u>Errors Allowed</u>—timings meeting the errors allowed will save (top three scores meeting the accuracy rate will always be saved). <u>Block Correction</u>—Disallow use of the backspace, delete, and arrow keys. <u>Blackout Timing View</u>—Blackens the timing screen until the timing is complete. <u>One Space / Two Space</u>—Set spacing after punctuation (".", ":", "!", "?").

TIMINGS	ERRORS ALLOWED	Block Correction	Blackout Timing View
15-Second	___	☐	☐
30-Second	___	☐	☐
1-Minute	___	☐	☐
2-Minute	___	☐	☐
3-Minute	___	☐	☐
4-Minute	___	☐	☐
5-Minute	___	☐	☐

● One Space　　○ Two Space　　| Advanced Options |

(1) Lock ID/Password: This disallows the changing of student ID/Passwords in the 'User Info' screen of the student program.
(2) Scores Required: Require students to have at least 1-3 scores recorded for each line in a lesson before marking the lesson complete. **Minimum WPM:** The minimum WPM threshold that recorded scores must meet to be saved for lesson averaging and grading purposes.
(3) Lesson Options: Enable/Disable lesson skipping.
(4) Text Options: Hide the text on screen. This can be used to teach touch typing, dictation typing, etc.

(1) ID/Password Changes

● ID/Password is NOT Locked (Default)

○ ID/Password is Locked

(3) Allow Lesson Skipping ☐

(2) Score Requirements

Scores required (Default is 1) ☐

Minimum WPM: ☐

(4) Hide Mastery Text ☐

SECTION E

This section contains the timing data for the optional timings. From the Main screen, select Optional Timings to take these timings. The progress reports and Final Grade Report will show the scores from these timings.

Double space between paragraphs (treat the timings as if they were single-spaced, always double space between single-spaced paragraphs).

Timing Weights: There are timings of different lengths in each lesson. Your instructor may feel that 1, 2, or 3 minute timings should be weighted more heavily for grading purposes than 15 or 30 second timings. These weights are all ratio based. In the example below, 15-sec. timings have a value of 1; 30-sec. timings are worth 2 times as much as 15-sec. timings; 1, 2, and 3 minute timings are worth 3 times as much as 15-second timings. The weighted lesson average will appear above each lesson on the *Progress Report*.

TIMINGS	TIMING WEIGHT	EXAMPLE
15-Second	___	1
30-Second	___	2
1-Minute	___	3
2-MInute	___	3
3-Minute	___	3
4-Minute	___	3
5-Minute	___	3

Sections: These are the lessons to be included in grading; weight them as a percentage of the total grade. This also allows the course to be individualized for students or classes. Any lessons with a weight of 0% (or blank) will not be used in the *Final Grade Report*.

LESSONS	% OF TOTAL GRADE	EXAMPLE
1 - 11 (Learning Keyboard)	___	40%
12 - 24 (Achieving Mastery)	___	40%
25 - 33 (Numbers & Symbols)	___	0%
Optional Timings		
1 - What Is a Clairvoyant? (3-min)	___	10%
2 - Life in the outback: Australia (3-min)	___	10%
3 - The Little Mermaid: Hans Christian (4-min)	___	0%
4 - What makes the holes in bread? (4-min)	___	0%
5 - How do animals communicate? (5-min)	___	0%
6 - What is intelligence? (5-min)	___	0%
7 - Who was Benedict Arnold? (5-min)	___	0%
8 - How to drink & never become an alcoholic (5-min)	___	0%
9 - Writing on clay tablets. (5-min)	___	0%
10 - The discovery of Penicillin. (5-min)	___	0%

18.   Inflation is what happens when prices in a
country rise so high and so quickly that they upset
the economy. Prices may start rising rapidly
because people want to buy more goods than there
are goods to go around. This is why goods cost so
much on the black market, or illegal market. Fears
of still higher prices may cause people to rush out
and buy things while they can still afford them.
Thus, the demand for goods increases and the cost
of them goes up even faster.

        One cure would be for people to stop buying.
However, it is difficult to persuade people to stop
buying things they want. Workers whose wages buy
them less, old people whose pensions are no longer
enough to live on, students whose grants no longer
support them, are all examples of people who press
for increased money to keep up with prices. Higher
wages most often mean higher prices for goods.

SETUP—Continued

Grading Scale: Enter the grading scale. This is measured in Words Per Minute (WPM). This will be used for both the current grade report and final grade report. The best timing for every lesson/line will be used for calculating the grade.

OVERALL AVERAGE WPM	GRADE	EXAMPLE
___	A	(35+)
___	B	(30)
___	C	(25)
___	D	(20)

Recap: The Recap screen shows you all the course standards that have been entered as a final check. If you have made an error, go back to the appropriate tab and enter the correct data. After you leave the *Setup*, **no changes can be made to the Name or ID.**

INTRODUCTION

Read each screen in the *Introduction*. Learn and practice the concepts explained in the S.E.C.R.E.T. to becoming a successful typist. Mastering these concepts will help you to gain high speeds with fewer errors.

In the introduction you will also practice: the home row, how timings work, additional features of the program, and you will take your first 15-second timing.

17.   The small hours are the early hours of the
morning from midnight until daybreak. They are the
times when most people are asleep. Some people find
that they do their best work if they can stay awake
past their normal bedtime when their bodies get
drowsy. Winston Churchill, the great British prime
minister, was such a person. He used to sleep for
an hour until midnight, and then hold his councils
of war in the small hours. Of course, this annoyed
no end his advisers who would rather have been
asleep.

        The end of the small hours in summer is the dawn
chorus when the birds wake each other up with their
songs.

LESSONS MENU

At the main screen, click on *Lessons Menu*. All the lessons will appear (*in demo/evaluation mode, not all lessons are available*). You will notice an empty box next to each lesson assigned in the Setup. This is lesson tracking. As each lesson is completed, a check mark will appear in the box.

Lesson timings can be printed by clicking on the printer icon after your timing has finished. This will print your name, ID, date/time, timing data keyed, errors underlined, WPM score, and errors made. This is especially helpful for in-class tests and may be required by your instructor to verify that students are 'doing their own work'. The printout may be compared to scores on the progress report.

If you already have some keyboarding skills you can take the **Course Entry** timing when starting the lessons and then take the **Course Exit** timing when finished. You will easily be able to see your skill improvements. **Course Entry** and **Course Exit** timings use Optional Timing 1 and Optional Timing 2, respectively, for these skill measurements if required.

Click on lesson '1 - Home Row', and practice to increase your score. Your best three scores will always show below the timing screen. Your best score that meets the accuracy rate will be used in grading.

The timer begins when the first key is pressed: If you complete the line before the timer stops you, press the Enter key and begin again on the <u>same</u> line. Keep typing until the timer stops you! If you 'mess up' and want to start over, just click on the Timer button to restart the timing. Single line timings do not word wrap. Press the Enter key twice after finishing a paragraph and start again—keep typing. Paragraph timings will word wrap, <u>use the Enter key twice between paragraphs and after finishing all paragraphs</u>—and then start again.

The *Progress Report* will show an asterisk by any score in which the correction key was used (if correction was allowed): If you are in a classroom situation, ask your instructor if you can use the Backspace key to correct errors. The asterisks will be ignored if you are allowed to use the correction key. Learn to use the correction key quickly and efficiently so you do not waste time and lower your speed score.

Optional Timings

Click on *Optional Timings* to open the optional timings list. You will notice a box next to each optional timing assigned in the setup; as each lesson is completed, a check mark appears.

Free Form

This allows you to be timed and receive a WPM score based on your own (or instructor-given) text. No error checking is performed since the program does not have your data. You will be prompted to enter the length of the timing and this timing may be printed for manual error checking.

10. lll >>> lll >>> l>l l>l ll> ll> >>l >>l l>l l>l >l>

11. b > a, d > c, f > e, g > h, j > i, mn > kl, qr > op

12. fuzzy > fizzy; pizzas > buzzard; tizzy > jazzy; z>y

30-Second Timings

13. If {their} was not the correct word, enter {there}.

14. Janeene thought that A < B and B < C. She is right.

15. If the angle AD > AB, then AC > AB; or so it seems.

1-Minute Timing   **S.I.—1.7**

16.   A madrigal is a song for several voices without
the support of a musical instrument. The madrigal
originated in Italy in the fourteenth century as a
short poem about love or the countryside, which was
then set to vocal music. It was customary for people
to entertain themselves at home by gathering around
a table and singing madrigals.

There are two types of progress reports, *Simple* and *Comprehensive*. *Simple Reports* show the highest score for each lesson line (if lessons are re-done, higher scores will replace lower scores). *Comprehensive Reports* show the top three scores for every timing. When a lesson is complete, the average score for that lesson will show below the lesson number. If correction is allowed in the Setup, asterisks (*) will indicate a correction key was used (Backspace, Delete, or Arrow keys). These reports can be printed by clicking on the printer icon. Below is a partial example of a *Simple Report*:

Keyboard Mastery—Progress Report

Opt. Timings 1: 33/1* 2: 41/0 3: 0/0 4: 0/0 5: 0/0 6: 0/0 7: 0/0 8: 0/0 9: 0/0 10: 0/0

Name: Audra Owens ID#: ao123   Date: 12/16/20xx   6:47 PM

Lesson Line Avg	1 42	2 40	3 41	4 42	5 41	6 42	7 44	8 46	9 46	10 43	11 45
1	36/0	40/1	41/0	39/0	41/1	29/0*	27/0*	28/0	25/0	21/1	39/0
2	40/0*	38/0	46/0	42/0	39/0	26/0*	29/0	33/0	31/0	22/0	50/1
3	39/0	38/0	39/0	44/0	45/0	32/0*	25/0	33/0*	36/1	30/0	48/0
4	39/0	39/0	35/0	40/0	47/1*	37/0*	31/0	30/0	29/1	29/0*	47/0
5	35/0	48/0	40/0*	39/0	40/0*	39/0	36/0	35/1	35/0	40/0	40/0
6	38/0	39/0	42/0*	50/1	48/0*	35/0	33/0	38/0	38/0	37/0	41/1
7	42/0	41/0	43/0	48/0	42/0	38/0	39/0	37/0	37/0*	40/1	44/0
8	38/0	39/0	39/0*	47/0	40/0	42/0	38/1*	40/0	40/0	42/1	39/0
9	42/0	42/0	40/0	40/0	43/0	45/0	40/0*	45/1	48/0	50/0	42/0
10	41/0	40/0	42/0	41/1	40/1*	43/0	49/1*	49/0	46/0	51/0*	40/0
11	46/0*	48/0	60/0	44/0	45/0	46/1	50/0	51/0	41/0	50/0	48/0
12	45/1*	40/0	59/0	59/0	41/2*	40/0	51/0	50/0	42/1*	45/0	40/0
13	31/0	41/2*	56/0	46/0	39/0	42/1	45/0	48/2	41/3*	40/0	41/2*
14	35/0	36/1	55/0	48/3	50/1	49/0	40/1	45/2	38/0	39/0	36/1
15	47/0	47/0	57/0	52/1	45/0	51/0	41/0	41/0	52/0	40/0	38/0
16	0/0	51/1	57/0	51/1*	38/0	43/0	40/0	40/0	51/0	41/2	38/0
17	0/0	53/0	59/0	62/0*	38/0	40/2	47/0*	47/3	47/1	41/2	39/0
18	0/0	58/1	61/1	65/1*	39/1	39/0	43/0*	45/3	46/0	42/1*	48/0

Lesson Line Avg	12 40	13 38	14 43	15 39	16 33	17 29	18 34	19 31	20 35	21 39	22 37
1	41/0	41/0	45/0	27/0*	29/0*	30/0	37/0	31/0	45/0	41/0	21/1
2	46/0	38/0	43/0	29/0	26/0*	29/0	40/0	36/0	43/0	46/0	22/0
3	39/0	45/0	46/1	25/0	32/0*	32/1	42/0*	33/0	46/1	39/0	30/0
4	35/0	48/0	40/0	31/0	37/0*	43/0	40/0	39/0	40/0	35/0	29/0*
5	40/0*	36/0	42/1	36/0	39/0	41/0	48/0	38/1*	42/1	40/0*	40/0
6	42/0*	46/0	49/0	33/0	35/0	46/0	40/0	40/0*	49/0	42/0*	37/0
7	43/0	41/0*	51/0	39/0	38/1	39/0	41/2*	49/1*	51/0	43/0	40/1
8	39/0*	50/0	43/0	40/0*	47/0	35/0	36/1	50/0	43/0	39/0*	42/1
9	45/1	51/1*	40/2	42/0*	45/1	40/0*	47/0	45/0	40/2	45/1	31/0
10	41/0*	43/2	39/0	43/0	48/0	42/0*	41/0*	43/0*	39/0	48/1	36/0
11	39/1	40/0*	51/1	39/0*	40/0	43/0	27/0*	48/0	27/0*	51/2	33/0
12	50/1	42/0*	48/0	40/0	41/2*	39/0*	29/0	40/0	29/0	59/0	39/0
13	45/0	43/0	40/0	42/0	36/1	40/0	25/0	41/2*	25/0	56/0	38/1*
14	40/0	39/0*	41/2*	60/0	38/0	48/0	31/0	36/1	31/0	55/0	40/0*
15	39/0	40/0	36/1	59/0	38/0	40/0	36/0	38/0	36/0	57/0	49/1*
16	40/0	42/0	38/0	45/1*	39/0	41/2*	33/0	38/0	33/0	57/0	50/0
17	41/0	60/0	38/0	40/1	48/0	36/1	39/0	39/0	39/0	59/0	51/0
18	44/0	59/0	39/1*	42/0	46/0	47/0	38/0*	48/0	41/1*	61/1	45/0

15-Second Warm-ups (Y and Z)

1. Guy yearned for a payday big enough to buy a yacht.

2. Twenty old junky taxis zipped along the slow zones.

3. A dozen citizens were amazed at the muzzled zebras.

Learn the '{ }' Keys   **Use ';' Finger, Shift of '[ ]' Keys**

4. ;{; ;{; {{; {{; ;;{ ;;{ {{; {{; ;{{ ;{{ ;;{ ;;{ {{;

5. ;}} ;}} }}; }}; ;}} ;}} ;;} ;;} };; };; ;}} ;}} }}}

6. year {{{ yours }}} yeast {{{ fuzzy }}} zeal {{{ zip

Learn the '<' Keys   **Use 'K' Finger, Shift of ',' Key**

7. kkk <<< kkk <<< k<k k<k <<k <<k k>> k>> k<k k<k <k<

8. a < b, c < d, e < f, g < h, i < j, kl < mn, op < qr

9. amaze < fizz; quick < zinc; zap < zip; zest < zone;

Grade Reports—Current Grade Report

The *Current Grade Report* shows the average WPM for all consecutively completed lessons. The final grade on the final grade report may differ slightly due to the weights of each section in the total grade (see 'Sections' in the Setup). If your current grade or final grade is not satisfactory to you, view your *Progress Report* to identify those timing scores that need more practice. A higher score will replace a lower score of the same lesson and line number. This report can be printed by clicking on the printer icon.

Keyboard Mastery—Current Grade Report

Name: Audra Owens   ID#: ao123   Date: 05/06/20xx   9:15 AM

```
Grading Scale:  40+    =    A

                35     =    B

                30     =    C

                25     =    D

                Below  =    F


        Your AVERAGE *UNWEIGHTED* WPM SCORE is: 44
This grade report is the average of 18 completed lessons.
```

18.   The modern custom of wearing gold wedding rings
originated in Roman times, but the idea took many
centuries to become established as a widely
accepted tradition. The first rings were made of
iron. The privilege of wearing gold rings was
reserved for Roman senators and magistrates.

As the Empire became more wealthy and
permissive, this right was allowed to spread
throughout the various levels of society. Engaged
couples took advantage of the freedom to use the
coveted gold for their wedding rings.

In English speaking countries, the wedding ring
is usually worn on the third finger of the left
hand. It was thought that a nerve ran from that
finger directly to the heart. However, in Germany
and France and other European countries, wedding
rings are worn on the third finger of the right
hand. The right hand is traditionally used for
making vows in these countries.

Grade Reports—Final Grade Report

The *Final Grade Report* shows the total weighted WPM for all completed lessons and sections. This final grade and WPM score may differ slightly from the *Current Grade Report* score due to weights being applied to section scores (see 'Sections' in the *Setup*). This report can be printed by clicking on the printer icon.

Keyboard Mastery—Evaluation and Grade Report

Name: Audra Owens   ** Final Timing Grade: A
ID#: ao123   Total Weighted WPM: 39
Time: 10:44 AM   ***All lessons assigned in the SETUP must be
Date: 05/06/20xx   completed before a final grade will appear.

Course Entry Score: 30 Course Exit Score: 44   Improvement: 14

Spacing: One Space   **Score Requirement:** 1   **Minimum WPM:** 10

Errors Allowed: 15-Sec. Timing = 0   **Block Correction:** 15-Second = Yes
                    30-Sec. Timing = 1   30-Second = Yes
                     1-Min. Timing = 1   1-Minute = No
                     2-Min. Timing = 2   2-Minute = No
                     3-Min. Timing = 3   3-Minute = No
                     4-Min. Timing = 4   4-Minute = No
                     5-Min. Timing = 5   5-Minute = No

Timing Weights: 15-Sec. Timing = 1
                    30-Sec. Timing = 2   **Grading Scale:**   35+   = A
                     1-Min. Timing = 3   30   = B
                     2-Min. Timing = 3   25   = C
                     3-Min. Timing = 3   20   = D
                     4-Min. Timing = 3   Below = F
                     5-Min. Timing = 3

Section	Avg. Score	X	% of Total	=	WPM Score
1—11 Learning Keyboard	40	X	30%	=	12
12—24 Learning Keyboard	44	X	30%	=	13.2
25-33 Numbers & Symbols	23	X	20%	=	4.6
Optional Timings (OT)					
1-What is a Clairvoyant?	46	X	10%	=	4.6
2-Life in the Outback: Australia.	43	X	10%	=	4.3
3-The Little Mermaid: Hans ...					
4-What makes holes in bread?					
5-How do animals communicate?					
6-What is intelligence?					
7-Who was Benedict Arnold?					
8-How to drink & never become...					
9-Writing on clay tablets.					
10-The discovery of penicillin.					

Total WPM: 38.7

16.   Albert Einstein is famous for his Theories of
Relativity which say that nothing in the universe is
absolutely still and that all motion is related.
Einstein worked out a method of measuring the speed
of moving objects. He used the three dimensions of
space--which is length, height, and thickness. He
added the fourth dimension of time. The three space
dimensions tell us where the object is, while the
fourth tells us when.

2-Minute Timing   S.I.—1.5

17.   Milk is pasteurized by heating it high enough to
kill most of the bacteria which causes milk to go
sour quickly, or cause disease in human beings. It
must be high enough to kill the tuberculosis
bacteria that used to kill millions of people of all
ages. At the same time, it must be low enough not to
alter the taste and quality of the milk too much.

        Pasteurized milk is much safer for babies than
untreated milk. In many countries it is the only
milk allowed to be sold. The process is named after
the French scientist, Louis Pasteur, whose
discoveries changed our knowledge about the effects
of bacteria.

SECTION ⓑ

Learning the Keyboard

10. ;+; ;+; ;++ ;++ ++; ++; ;+; ;+; ;;+ ;;+ +;; +;; ;+;

11. ;[+ ;[+ ;++ ;++ ;[+ ;[+ +[; +[; ;++ ;++ ;+; ;+; ;++

12. wet +++ wild +++ wax +++ war +++ wise +++ wants +++

30-Second Timings

13. The = and + signs are mostly used in math problems.

14. The computer program listed an equation of A+B+C=D.

15. A = B + C is a standard equation in their programs.

REVIEW—WHAT IS THE 'HOME ROW'?

The four fingers of your left hand covers the **a s d f**
- The little finger should be on the 'a' and the next finger on the 's', and so forth.

The four fingers of your right hand covers the **j k l ;**
- The little finger should be on the ';' and the next finger on the 'l', and so forth.

Place your fingers on the home row now. Do your fingers look like the picture below?

15-Second Timings

The timing will begin when you strike the first key. If you 'mess up' and want to begin again, click on the timer button. You may take the timings as many times as necessary. If you finish the line before the time is up, press the 'Enter' key and start the line again.

1. aaa sss ddd fff jjj kkk lll ;;; fff jjj ddd kkk

2. aaa sss kkk ask ask sss aaa ddd sad sad ask sad

3. ddd aaa ddd dad dad lll aaa ddd lad lad dad lad

4. aaa ddd add add fff aaa ddd fad fad add fad dad

5. jjj aaa lll ddd kkk sss aaa ;;; lll jjj fff ddd

15-Second Warm-ups (V, W, and X)

1. Vinni visited a revival and was very visibly moved.

2. Will was an awkward waif who wanted wages to write.

3. Mixi has exactly six extra boxes of texts on taxes.

Learn the '=' Key   **Reach with the ';' Finger**

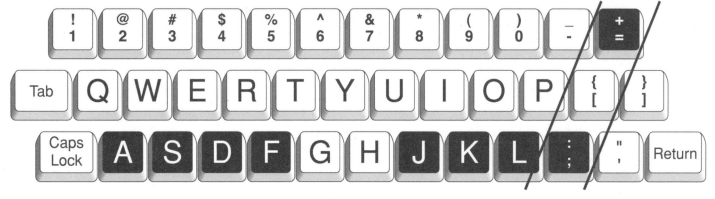

4. ;=; ;=; ==; ==; ;;= ;;= ;=; ;=; ==; ==; ;== ;== ;=;

5. ;;= ;;= =;= =;= ;;= ;;= =;; =;; ;=; ;=; ;;= ;;= =;=

6. sixty === exam === extent === expand === extras ===

Learn the '[ ]' Keys   **Reach with the ';' Finger**

7. ppp [[[ ]]] ppp [[[ ]]] ppp [[[ ]]] ppp [[[ ]]] ppp

8. [a] [a] [s] [s] [d] [d] [f] [f] [a] [a] [s] [s] [d]

9. [[[vice]]] very [[[vase]]] vast [[[veto]]] [[

30-Second Timings

- Don't rest your hands on the keyboard or desk! Your arms and wrists should be straight.
- Can you press the 'Enter' key and keep typing without taking your eyes off the copy?
- Are you using the same thumb to press the space bar?

```
6.  ddd daa dad dll dll jaa jaa lss lss las las add

7.  sss aaa ddd sad sad lll aaa ddd lad lad sad lad

8.  aaa ddd add add fff aaa ddd fad fad add dad fad

9.  daa daa la; la; jaa aaa lss dss sss dad dad dss

10. aaa lll all all jal jal las las sks sks kff kff
```

1-Minute Timings

```
11. ddd add dad fdd fad sad sad ask ask las las slk

12. jaj jaj kdk kdk dss dss l;; l;; ;a; ;a; jaa jaa

13. sas sas fds fds jkl jkl asd asd kl; kl; faf faf

14. aka aka ;l; ;l; fjf fjf dkd dkd sls sls ;as ;as

15. all all sal sal jal jal kad kad das das jak jak
```

Keyboard Mastery—Progress Report

Opt. Timings 1: 33/1* 2: 41/0 3: 0/0 4: 0/0 5: 0/0 6: 0/0 7: 0/0 8: 0/0 9: 0/0 10: 0/0

Name: Audra Owens ID#: ao123   Date: 12/16/20xx   6:47 PM

Lesson	1	2	3	4	5	6	7	8	9	10	11
Line Avg	42	40	41	42	41	42	44	46	46	43	45
1	36/0	40/1	41/0	39/0	41/1	29/0*	27/0*	28/0	25/0	21/1	39/0
2	40/0*	38/0	46/0	42/0	39/0	26/0*	29/0	33/0	31/0	22/0	50/1
3	39/0	38/0	39/0	44/0	45/0	32/0*	25/0	33/0*	36/1	30/0	48/0
4	39/0	39/0	35/0	40/0	47/1*	37/0*	31/0	30/0	29/1	29/0*	47/0
13	31/0						45/0	48/2	41/3*	40/0	41/2*
14	35/0						40/1	45/2	38/0	39/0	36/1
15	47/0						41/0	41/0	52/0	40/0	38/0
16	0/0						40/0	40/0	51/0	41/2	38/0
17	0/0						47/0*	47/3	47/1	41/2	39/0
18	0/0	58/1	61/1	65/1*	39/1	39/0	43/0*	45/3	46/0	42/1*	48/0

Note: Some lessons do not have 18 lines, therefore, 0/0 will appear on the Progress Reports. This will in no way affect the lesson averages or final grade.

18.   It is believed that the Babylonians first used
a pole fixed in the ground to measure the passing
of time. They noticed that the position of the
shadow changed during the hours of sunlight. They
found that the shadow was long at sunrise and that
it slowly grew shorter until it reached a point
when it started to lengthen again. They noticed
that at sunset the shadow was as long as it was at
sunrise.

       The simple shadow and pole arrangement was the
basis of the various shadow clocks or sundials used
by the ancient Egyptians. Eventually, sundials were
provided with the hour figures engraved on a metal
plate. The Egyptians also used a water clock. This
was a basin-shaped, alabaster vessel filled with
water that ran out through a hole in the bottom.
The time was indicated by the level of water
remaining inside. Monks were the first to operate
clocks by wheels and weights. Clocks of this type,
found in monasteries, date back to the fourteenth
century. The first spring clock appeared in about
the fifteenth century.

15-Second Warm-ups

- Fast typists tap the keys with a sharp, quick stroke—as if the keys were hot. Don't mash the keys.
- Keep typing at a steady pace—try to eliminate pauses. Your speed will improve.

1. all all add add sad sad ask ask fad fad lad lad

2. dad dad las las kad kad sal sal fas fas ;sf ;sf

3. a sad dad; a sad lass; ask a lad; ask all lads;

Learn the 'T' Key   **Reach with the 'F' finger**

When your 'f' finger reaches to strike the 't' key, the other fingers should remain on the home row.

4. fff ttt fff ttt ftf ftf fat fat sat sat tal tal

5. tat tat tad tad fad fad tas tas tft tft jft jft

6. lat lat jat jat dat dat klt klt ;lt ;lt flt flt

Learn the 'E' Key   **Reach with the 'D' finger**

When your 'd' finger reaches to strike the 'e' key, your 'f' finger may go up too, but the rest of your fingers should remain on the home row. Always have some fingers on the home row as a guide for returning fingers.

7. ddd eee ddd eee ded ded ede ede dee dee edd edd

8. ded ded tee tee let let set set fed fed led led

9. dek dek jet jet jel jel tel tel fat fat tea tea

30-Second Timings

(Make a solid line by pressing the Underscore key the number of times indicated in parenthesis—without any spaces between.)

13. Name _____(12)_____ Date _____(12)_____ Period ___(8)___

14. Marge (the wife) and Sam (the husband) like skiing.

15. Jill (first base) and Barbara (pitcher) can't come.

1-Minute Timing   S.I.—1.6

16.   Concrete can be said to have been used for
    thousands of years, if the word is taken generally to
    mean a hard building material produced from a mixture
    of cement, sand, gravel, and stone. The Assyrians and
    Babylonians used clay to bind sand and stones, and
    the ancient Egyptians discovered lime and gypsum.
    The Romans mixed slaked lime with volcanic ash and
    constructed aqueducts, bridges, and buildings.

2-Minute Timing   S.I.—1.3

17.   Plasma is the liquid part of the blood in which
    the red and white blood cells float. The red cells
    carry oxygen and give the blood its red color. The
    plasma itself looks like the color of straw. You may
    have seen some oozing out around a burn or cut.

        Along with red cells, the plasma helps to carry
    oxygen from the lungs to the body tissues. When the
    tissues have finished with the oxygen, the blood
    carries the carbon dioxide waste back to the lungs in
    order for it to be breathed out. It also carries
    food, at various stages of absorption, to the body
    tissues and takes the waste away to the kidneys to be
    passed out of the body.

Learn the 'H' Key   **Reach with the 'J' finger**

Keep your fingers curved on the home row keys. Straighten the 'J' finger to tap the 'H' key. Let the finger do the reaching—always keep some fingers on the home row.

10. jjj hhh jjj hhh jhj jhj hjh hjh hat hat the the

11. hah hah haj haj the the hel hel seh seh kah kah

12. hal hal teh teh had had jhj jhj aha aha has has

30-Second Timings

13. ftf ftf tale tale test test sets sets tall tall

14. daf daf jak jak lad lad ;th ;th fkl fkl ;a; ;a;

15. fad fad lad lad salad salad had had the del del

1-Minute Timings

16. ask a dad; ask a tall lad; she sees a tall shed;

17. the lads ate a salad; the lads had a tall salad;

18. the sales tell a sad tale; the tall lad had sat;

Learn the ')' Key   **Use the ';' Finger, Shift of '0' Key**

7. ;;;))) ;;;))) ;); ;); ;;) ;;)));)); ;); ;);)))

8. ;p) ;p) p)) p)) ;p) ;p)))p))p ;)) ;)) ;p) ;p)));

9. pick))) pal))) print))) pole))) pit))) pie)))

Learn the '_' Key   **Use the ';' Finger, Shift of '0' Key**

(The broken underscores have spaces between them.)

10. _ _ _ ;;; _ _ _ ;;; _ _ _ ;_; ;_; ;;_ ;;_ _;_ _;_ ;

11. ;p_ ;p_ p_p p_p ;p_ ;p_ pp_ pp_ ;p_ ;p_ pp_ pp_ p_p

12. Name _ _ _ Date _ _ _ Class _ _ _ Teacher _ _ _ _ _

15-Second Warm-ups

1. the the sad sad let let ask ask tel tel lad lad

2. the dad sees the sad lads; he asks the sad lad;

3. a fad; ask dad; she sees the lads; the sad dad;

Learn the 'O' Key   **Reach with the 'L' finger**

4. lll ooo lll ooo lol lol ool ool old old lol lol

5. sod sod old old oh; oh; odd odd hod hod off off

6. she held a solo; the odd lad has to sell shoes;

Learn the 'R' Key   **Reach with the 'F' finger**

7. fff rrr fff rrr frf frf rff rff frr frr fro fro

8. red red era era ark ark her her oar oar are are

9. he offered her a red jar; he took the rare oar;

15-Second Warm-ups (S, T, and U)

1. A desperate suspect urged the stern typist to stop.

2. The untimely union of the town seemed to be useful.

3. Top guides have taught values to thousands of kids.

Learn the '(' Key   **Use 'L' Finger, Shift of '9' Key**

4. lll (((lll (((l(l l(l ((l ((l ll(ll(l(l l(l (9(

5. lo(lo((ol (ol ((o ((o oo(oo(((l ((l ll(ll(oo(

6. lull (((like (((lull (((legal (((locate (((lit

10. jjj nnn jjj nnn jnj jnj njj njj jnj jnj fan fan

11. and and sand sand den den dent dent tan tan net

12. ten tall lads lent a note; the tent has snakes;

30-Second Timings

Be sure to press the 'Enter/Return' key without taking your eyes off the textbook! Try to keep a steady rhythm—no pauses!

13. sand sand land land snakes snakes land land she

14. her her heard heard off off told told sent sent

15. roll rolled told told dad dad asked asked raked

1-Minute Timings

16. she heard the lads ask for a roll; she ate too;

17. she told the lad not to fall; then he fell off;

18. he sent the snakes off and then raked the land;

---

18.   Hard water is water that contains certain
dissolved minerals that act on soap to form a
deposit known as scum. If water comes from
limestone areas, some rock is dissolved in the
water and this makes it hard.

        There are several disadvantages in using hard
water. More soap or soap powder must be used to
obtain a suitable lather. Also, the scum clings to
the object being washed. Hard water leaves a scaly
deposit in kettles and boilers which looks bad and
reduces the efficiency of both. Cleaning showers,
tubs, sinks, and commodes are more difficult
because of mineral deposits that stick to the
surfaces.

        However, hard water can be treated to remove
the unwanted chemicals. In the home, small amounts
of washing soda or borax can be added. At large
water softening plants which serve a community, the
water is filtered through a mineral called zeolite
that removes the chemicals.

15-Second Warm-ups

1. rear rear neat neat raft raft shoe shoe old old

2. rolls rolls dad dad ask ask doe doe for for fed

3. she fed a doe; she heard dad ask for the rolls;

Learn the 'M' Key   **Reach with the 'J' finger**

4. mmm jjj mmm jjj mjm mjm jmj jmj jam jam mam mam

5. mar mar ham ham ma; ma; dam dam mom mom mad mad

6. mom made room for her jams; she looked for ham;

Learn the 'C' Key   **Reach with the 'D' finger**

7. ccc ddd ccc ddd cdc cdc dcc dcc dcd dcd cde cde

8. cot cot cat cat can can catch catch ace ace car

9. her cats can also catch cod; she can see cakes;

30-Second Timings

13. Casey & Jane & Bill will buy all the stock on sale.

14. Darner & Plymouth will merge with Johnson & Smiley.

15. Please identify the following: 115*, 20*, and 328*.

1-Minute Timing   S.I.—1.5

16.   Meteorites begin as bodies of matter traveling
     at great speeds through space. In the solar system
     they are numberless and are usually chunks of rock
     or metal. When they enter the atmosphere, friction
     makes them hot and bright. The small chunks burn
     away, but the larger ones fall to the earth as
     meteorites.

2-Minute Timing   S.I.—1.5

17.   The exact time the first wristwatch was made is
     now known. Soon after the beginning of the twentieth
     century, small pocket watches for women began to be
     made on leather or gold to be worn on the wrist.
     They were immediately successful, and their
     popularity rapidly increased in the First World War
     because women could tell time without undoing a coat
     or uniform.

         The first self-winding wristwatch was invented
     by John Harwood, an Englishman, who received a
     patent in 1924. Today, the largest watchmaking
     industry in the world is concentrated in the Jura
     mountains and the valley of the AAr in Switzerland.

Learn the Left Shift Key   **Reach with the 'A' finger**

Place your left hand on the home row. Keep your 'F' finger lightly on the 'F' key while you use your 'A' finger to hold down the Left Shift key; with the Left Shift key down, press the 'J' key with the right hand. Return the left hand to its home row position. When the Shift key is down, and a letter key is pressed, it makes a capital letter. Why do you think it is important to leave the 'F' finger on its home row position while you press the Shift key?

10. JJJ jjj KKK kkk LLL lll OOO ooo NNN nnn HHH hhh

11. Lands Lands Hal Hal Lee Lee Karen Karen jJj jJj

12. He can see the land; and Karen can also see her

30-Second Timings

13. Hal and Lee call at the store; he can cook corn

14. Her date aces the test; He took oak to the farm

15. Ken can call the class off; Jack can not cease;

1-Minute Timings

16. Kas and Ken are men; He can see her at the dam;

17. Lead me to Lad; He cannot see the old oak tree;

18. Karen shall meet me at the old salt flat at ten

Learn the '&' Key   **Use the 'J' Finger, Shift of '7' Key**

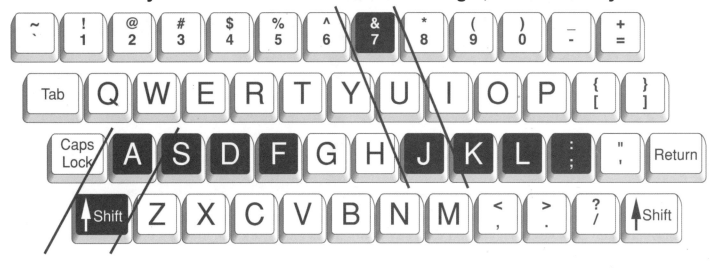

7. jjj &&& jjj &&& j&j j&j jj& jj& &&j &&j j&j j&j &&j

8. ju& ju& u&& u&& &&u &&u &&j &&j j&& j&& ju& ju& &uj

9. junk &&& jobs &&& jumbo &&& jewel &&& juror &&& jet

Learn the '*' Key   **Use the 'K' Finger, Shift of '8' Key**

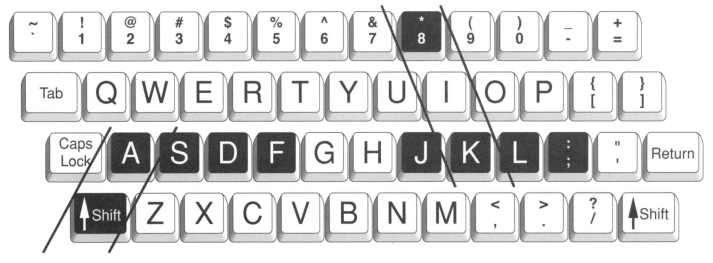

10. *** kkk *** kkk k*k k*k **k **k k*k k*k kk* kk* k*k

11. ki* ki* *ik *ik k*k k*k i*i i*i *k* *k* ki* ki* kk*

12. kicks *** cook *** kink *** knack *** kayak *** kin

The **S.E.C.R.E.T.** to Successful Keyboarding Skills

S — SIT upright, arms and wrists straight.

E — Keep your EYES on the copy.

C — Use CORRECT fingers. Keep fingers near the home row.

R — Keep a reasonable RHYTHM.

E — Eliminate ERRORS properly.
> If your teacher allows error correction, keep your 'J' finger on the 'J' key while your little finger depresses the 'backspace' key.

T — TAP your keys as if they were hot!

15-Second Warm-ups (P, Q, and R)

1. Peter performed with poise on the plywood platform.

2. The queen ate squab and squid acquired in quantity.

3. There were rows and rows of ravens near the barges.

Learn the '^' Key   **Use 'J' Finger, Shift of '6' Key**

4. jjj ^^^ jjj ^^^ j^j j^j ^^j ^^j j^j j^j jj^ jj^ j^j

5. jy^ jy^ yy^ yy^ y^^ y^^ y^y y^y ^^y ^^y jy^ jy^ ^y^

6. jack ^^^ jaws ^^^ jolly ^^^ jury ^^^ juicy ^^^ jots

Lesson 5   I, Period, and Right Shift

15-Second Warm-ups

1. add odd foods to the salad; take notes on jokes

2. the host took the folks to one of the old oaks;

3. she told the host that the food can stand here;

Learn the 'I' Key   Reach with the 'K' finger

4. iii kkk iii kkk kit kit sit sit fin fin aid aid

5. sift sift list list said said hit hit lids lids

6. the kids took the kite; the kids are not still;

Learn the '.' Key   Reach with the 'L' finger

7. lll ... lll ... l.l l.l .ll .ll .l. .l. l.l l.l

18.   A magnet is a piece of iron which will attract
or repel pins, tacks, nails or anything else made
of that metal. The word comes from a district in
Thessaly, Greece, called Magnesia. It was here that
men first noticed that certain black stones
attracted iron. These stones were composed of an
iron ore called magnetite, and were natural
magnets.

        Later, it was discovered that if a piece of
magnetite or lodestone was hung by a thread or
floated on a piece of wood, it would always turn to
point north and south. This proved very useful to
the early sailors.

        Next, it was found that a magnet could be made
by winding an insulated wire around a piece of iron
and passing an electric current through the wire.
This is called an electromagnet and is used in an
electric motor. Magnets can be made by stroking a
piece of iron with lodestone, or with another
magnet, which passes on the power of magnetism.

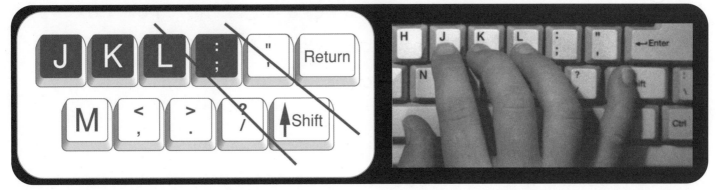

Place your right hand on the home row. Keep your 'J' finger lightly on the 'J' key while you lift up your ';' finger and hold down the Right Shift key. Type a letter with the left hand. <u>Always leave the 'J' finger in place as a guide so the fingers can return to the home row easily</u>. This is how you make capital letters with the left hand.

Depending on the setup, you will space once or twice after a period between sentences.

8. Joel is late. The thief left the dinner at one.

9. Lon took the kite as a joke; I did not like it.

10. Ada Ada Dale Dale The The dad dad Fred Fred Sam

11. Ada read the tale to Dale and Fred; Sam did it.

12. Deena is not inside. Dale made her read it all.

30-Second Timings

13. She heard the man ask for a roll. Jacki ate it.

14. Dr. Todd asked for nine rakes; there are three.

15. The three rolls of dimes are for Dona and Cher.

1-Minute Timings

16. The old farmers deeded the ranches to the sons.

17. Traci races small cars on the tracks at school.

18. Dale hired the jet to take him home after jail.

30-Second Timings

13. One #2 and two #3 pencils were missing from box #5.

14. The amount of the invoices were $12.00 and $113.00.

15. The terms were 10% discount if paid within 15 days.

1-Minute Timing   S.I.—1.4

16.   A legend says that the coffee plant first grew in
Ethiopia, where it was discovered by a goatherd about
the year 850. Goats were reported to have skipped and
pranced in a strange manner after feeding on a
certain evergreen plant. The goatherd, so the story
goes, tried some of the berries himself and excitedly
dashed to the nearest town to tell of his find. It
was called coffee after the name of the province.

2-Minute Timing   S.I.—1.5

17.   Objects will appear reversed in a mirror because
what you are seeing is a reflection and not an actual
reproduction of the image. If you stand in front of a
mirror with your right eye closed, the image in the
mirror will appear to show your left eye closed
because the image is facing the opposite direction.

        By using a combination of two mirrors at right
angles to each other, the image reversal will be
eliminated. This is because the reversed image will
be reversed yet again in the second mirror, thus
giving a true likeness of the original object. So, if
you want to see what you really look like, look into
the corner of two mirrors at right angles to each
other.

15-Second Warm-ups

1. Janet Janet sell sell none none late late test test

2. too too failed failed Lin Lin dinner dinner the the

3. Janet is too late for dinner. Linn failed the test.

Learn the Comma ',' Key   **Reach with the 'K' finger**

4. kkk ,,, kkk ,,, k,k k,k ki, ki, ,k, ,k, kids, kids,

5. letters, letters, folders, folders, checks, checks,

6. He had letters, folders, and one check in his desk.

Learn the 'U' Key   **Reach with the 'J' finger**

7. uuu jjj uuu jjj uju uju juj juj juu juu uju uju huj

8. just just junk junk must must under under uses uses

9. To eat food here, at least clean under the old mat.

Learn the '$' Key   **Use the 'F' Finger, Shift of '4' Key**

7. fff $$$ fff $$$ f$f f$f ff$ ff$ $$f $$f f$f f$f $$f

8. fr$ fr$ $rf $rf r$$ r$$ rr$ rr$ fr$ fr$ r r $$$

9. $$$ fair $$$ frill $$$ fried $$$ offer $$$ muff $$$

Learn the '%' Key   **Use the 'F' Finger, Shift of '5' Key**

10. fff %%% fff %%% f%f f%f ff% ff% %%f %%f %f% %f% %ff

11. fr% fr% rr% rr% fr% fr% %%r %%r %r% %r% fr% fr% %rf

12. %%% fade %%% fable %%% buff %%% frail %%% forks %%%

Learn the 'Caps Lock' Key   Reach with the 'A' finger

The Caps Lock key is a toggle key—meaning that if you press it down, it is on; if you press it again, it is off; if you press it again, it is on; etc.

When you have several characters or words that you want in all capital letters, press the Caps Lock key down, type them, and press the Caps Lock key again to turn it off for regular typing.

10. The name of it is THE CASES OF THE SCARED CHILDREN.

11. RED AND READ sound similar; this can cause concern.

12. Don is sick. CURTIS IS NOT SICK; he just acts sick.

30-Second Timings

13. Take ten, let three stand; these are a fresh start.

14. Arni has landed the jet; Uri is just third in line.

15. THE LAST TALES is a fine one, and I should read it.

1-Minute Timings

16. She took old junk out from under the old tree fort.

17. Our uncle forced Dan to eat corn, our aunt did not.

18. Corn is a common food. Salads and fish are less so.

15-Second Warm-ups (M, N, and O)

1. Mary and Mike made amends for smashing nine melons.

2. The nice nanny sang songs and made winning dinners.

3. Take the onions and olives from the omelet and eat.

Learn the '#' Key   **Use 'D' Finger, Shift of '3' Key**

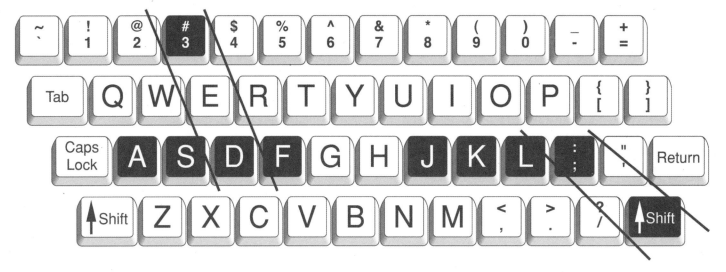

4. ddd ### ddd ### d## d## ##d ##d d#d d#d D#D D#D d#d

5. de# de# #ed #ed e#e e#e #ed #ed #ee #ee #e# #e# de#

6. ### drink ### dream ### dead ### dome ### deers ###

15-Second Warm-ups

1. Lester Lester under under that that sales sales it

2. small small said said here here June June are less

3. Lester said that the sales for June are much less.

Learn the 'B' Key   **Reach with the 'F' finger**

4. bbb fff bbb fff bfb bfb fbf fbf rib rib bat bat bif

5. bit bit bank bank bob bob bar bar fib fib brat brat

6. A bank is robbed. Janice asked the bar for a drink.

Learn the 'P' Key   **Reach with the ';' finger**

7. ;;; ppp ;;; ppp ;p; ;p; pie pie pan pan pen pen pal

8. Put Put about about special special paper paper pen

9. Put pencil to paper to tell about special problems.

18.   Voodoo, or Vodun, meaning spirit, is an African
name given to rites practiced in very poor areas of
Haiti. It was developed by African slaves brought to
the island by the French during the late seventeenth
century and has now spread to Cuba, Jamaica, and
Brazil.

      Possessing no defined doctrine, Voodoo is very
elastic and flexible to mean anything people want it
to mean. As any primitive religion demands, it is
full of myths and magic. Beliefs are so strong that
if someone is cursed with a sharp bone, and the
curse is found out, he or she goes into their living
quarters, lays down, and dies. Since most of the
Voodooists are also Roman Catholics, they have
introduced many of the church's beliefs into their
religion. For instance, they have enthusiastically
adopted many saints. However, when babies are
baptized, they are thrown through flames so as to
become fortified against danger.

      Ritual dances occupy an important part of their
lives and usually take place in the presence of a
priest or priestess. These dances are rhythmic and
are accompanied by drums. Back and forth the dancers
shuffle, shoulders shaking and eyes rolling as they
chant incomprehensible words.

Learn the 'W' Key   **Reach with the 'S' finger**

10. sss www sss www sws sws saw saw was was how how now

11. William William work work Jo Jo wanted wanted hard.

12. William wanted to work with Jo, but it is too hard.

30-Second Timings

13. Our audit should now be as planned; it is not poor.

14. The truth must come out before we do those windows.

15. Rub the rust from under the cars, and sweep it off.

1-Minute Timings

16. A desk has three drawers for new credit card bills.

17. The police were prompt when called, but he ran off.

   Space once after a period used in an abbreviation such as Mr. or Mrs. or Dr.

18. Ms. White had a pink sport coat; Mr. White had red.

16.   You should not watch television in a darkened
           room because the picture will not be as clear as
           when there is a little background light. Viewing in
           a dark room can cause an unpleasant glare from the
           screen; it also intensifies the normal flickering
           that can cause eye fatigue. If the screen is too
           bright, light can be reflected onto the retina of
           the eye and produce the same effect as looking at
           the bright lights of an oncoming car.

17.   Hypnotism is the art of putting the brain of a
           patient into a trance-like state which the
           hypnotist can then control. It is a way of exploring
           the deeper areas of the mind and possibly releasing
           a patient from unconscious fears, worries, and
           strains.

           For hypnotism to succeed, the patient must trust
           and cooperate. Once the patient is in a trance, the
           mind returns to a more simple, childlike state. The
           patient often remembers incidents that happened
           when very young, incidents which may have affected
           the personality. The hypnotist, who should also be a
           trained doctor, will be in a position to help him or
           her to understand those fears.

15-Second Warm-ups

1. We were told to take a train to Prescott and soon.

2. Ted came to town to see soccer; it was rained out.

3. Dot said the sale was lost before he came to town.

Learn the 'G' Key   **Reach with the 'F' finger**

4. fff ggg fff ggg fgf fgf gfg gfg fff ggg fgf got got

5. He He Leg Leg eggs eggs snagged snagged broke broke

6. He got his leg snagged in the logs. The eggs broke.

Learn the ':' Key   **Reach with the Shift and the ';' finger**

Notice that the ':' and ';' are both on the same key. When there are two options on one key, the top one is obtained by using the shift key. Depending on the 'Setup', you may be asked to press the spacebar once (default) or twice after a colon.

7. ;;; ::: ;;; ::: ;:; ;:; ::; ::; ;;: ;;: ::: ;;; :::

8. Mr. Smith: Dear Mr. Smith: Mrs. Lee: Dear Mrs. Lee:

9. The memo reads To: Mr. Greener; From: Mrs. Greener;

8. aq! aq! !qa !qa !q! !q! aq! aq! !a! !a! !qa !qa aq!

Line 9 is a sentence. Depending on the SETUP you will need 1 or 2 spaces after an Exclamation mark (hint: Remember, press 'Enter' after the end of a sentence—no spaces).

9. Help! Those pirates are coming! Get out the cannon!

Learn the '@' Key   **Use 'S' Finger, Shift of '2' Key**

10. sss @@@ sss @@@ s@s s@s @@s @@s ss@ ss@ sss @@@ s@s

11. sw@ sw@ @ws @ws sw@ sw@ @w@ @w@ @@w @@w ww@ ww@ sw@

12. 75 @@@ 36 @@@ 95 @@@ 72 @@@ 30 @@@ 59 @@@ 60 @@@ 14

30-Second Timings

13. Our new stock grew from 300 @ 4 1/2 to 550 @ 7 7/8.

(Hint: Remember, depending on the SETUP you will need 1 or 2 spaces after a colon)

14. Buy now at these times: 24 @ 12 1/2 and 15 @ 6 3/4.

15. We bought 8 @ 8 1/2, and waited to sell 5 @ 18 1/2.

10. aaa qqq aaa qqq aqa aqa qqa qqa qaq qaq aqq aqq qqa

11. Quick Quick wink wink people people quieter quieter

12. Quick as a wink, people are going about their jobs.

30-Second Timings

13. Dear Frank: I am going abroad for awhile; how nice.

14. Gregg cannot be quiet: please come and get him now.

15. Tammi: I am coming to classes now. I will see Cher.

1-Minute Timings

16. Staci: I am going to go to the HAUNTED HOUSE ATTIC.

17. Annie cannot quit quipping without getting mad too.

18. Wanda will want to equip the tent with bug killers.

15-Second Warm-ups (J, K, and L)

1. The 197 joggers had 33 jars of jam at the jamboree.

2. Can Kate make 8 kilts and 17 khakis in the kickoff?

3. Lyle has 25 legal and lawful complaints to fulfill.

Learn the '0' Key   **Reach with the ';' finger**

4. ;;; 000 ;;; 000 ;0; ;0; 00; 00; ;;0 ;;0 ;;; 000 ;;;

5. ;p0 ;p0 pp0 pp0 0p0 0p0 00p 00p 0p; 0p; ;00 ;00 00;

6. 20 time 30 seat 60 real 80 forty 70 diner 40 called

Learn the '!' Key   **Use 'A' Finger, Shift of '1' Key**

7. aaa 111 !!! aaa 111 !!! a1! a1! !!a !!a 1a! 1a! q!!

15-Second Warm-ups

1. She can ski down that hill, but I would rather not.

2. The father liked to read to his children at nights.

3. Eight sail boats are for sale. The bankers own one.

Learn the 'V' Key   **Reach with the 'F' finger**

4. fff vvv fff vvv fvf fvf vff vff fvf fvf fvv fvv vfv

5. Levi Levi moved moved evening evening Val left left

6. Jan cried; Levi moved; and Vicki left this evening.

Learn the '/' Key   **Reach with ';' finger**

7. ;;; /// ;;; /// ;/; ;/; /// ;;; /;/ /;/ ;;; ;/; ;/;

8. off/on off/on pass/fail pass/fail audit/credits no/

9. An off/on selection is not good; choose true/false.

18.   When you yawn, or when you see somebody else do it, it is a sign of a need for more oxygen in your lungs. When you have been sitting in a room where the air has become stale, your body cries out for oxygen to cleanse and purify your blood. The quickest way to supply that need is to open the mouth wide and breathe in air.

   Better still, you should get out into the fresh air and breathe deeply. You will then find that the need to yawn will vanish because you are getting a better supply of oxygen. Why should you yawn when you are bored? You are probably not breathing deeply and feeding your lungs as you should. Of course, the ideal cure is to escape from what is boring you. If that is not possible, try breathing deeply.

   You have probably noticed that you sometimes yawn when you are tired. This means your body cells need renewal with oxygen. Going to sleep not only rests the body, but it sets up deep rhythmic breathing which satisfies the hunger for oxygen.

Learn the '?' Key   **Hold Left Shift key down, press '/'**

Hold the left shift key down while you press the '/' key, then raise the left shift key finger quickly and keep going.

10. ??? ;;; ??? ;;; ;?; ;?; ??? ;;; ?;; ?;; ;?? ;?? ?;?

Depending on the setup, you will space once (default) or twice after a question mark (?).

11. Will Tara be going? How will she be going? Is Chad?

12. Are the answers off/on or t/f? Or is there another?

30-Second Timings

13. Vicki voted for him. How would Joan vote on it now?

14. Are these rules too hard? Get David to change them.

15. That in/out basket is full. Is the off/on valve on?

1-Minute Timings

16. Tom said that it became evident that it was vulgar.

17. These are the pass/fail rules: twice means failure?

18. What did Anne do to them? She said it, then did it.

---

17.   Genghis Khan was a Mongolian who was born in the
eleventh century in northern China. As a boy he was
named Temujin, but he grew up to be such an able
soldier that he was named Genghis Khan by his many
followers. The new name probably meant Ocean Chief,
using the word ocean as meaning wide or
encompassing.

        A series of conquests made him undisputed
leader of all the nomad or wandering tribes in his
area. His ferocity became a byword because he used
living citizens as shield walls for his troops. He
often deliberately massacred thousands of prisoners
to frighten cities into surrendering.

15-Second Warm-ups

1. He had to quit his potato packaging labor in Idaho.

2. She will not follow his spelling programs in class.

3. Is Linda here? Her sons were still looking for her.

Learn the 'X' Key   **Reach with the 'S' finger**

4. sss xxx sss xxx sxs sxs ssx ssx xsx xsx sxs sxs xss

5. fox fox six six lax lax wax wax box box nix nix axe

6. The fox grabbed the six chicks. The farmer was lax.

Learn the 'Y' Key   **Reach with 'J' finger**

7. jjj yyy jjj yyy jyj jyj jay jay yjy yjy jyj jyj yjj

8. year year Andy Andy stayed stayed yard yard big big

9. Last year Andy stayed behind to clean the big yard.

10. lll 999 lll 999 l9l l9l ll9 ll9 99l 99l lll 999 l9l

11. lo9 lo9 9ol 9ol oo9 oo9 99o 99o o9o o9o 9ol 9ol l9l

12. 91 lass 992 call 993 lazy 994 life 995 lull 996 lot

30-Second Timings

13. The real amount of time was 239 minutes and 51 sec.

14. Item numbers 3639 and 7471 were not delivered then.

15. Call in and order 59 pens, 35 folders, and 7 chalk.

1-Minute Timing   **S.I.—1.4**

16.   The Black Death was a plague that raged through Europe during the thirteenth century. It was caused by fleas living on rats which were carried there from Asia by trading ships. It is suggested that the Black Death was probably Bubonic Plague. About one in three Europeans died of the disease.

10. aaa zzz aaa zzz aza aza zaz zaz aaa azz azz aza aza

11. size size pizza pizza amazed amazed zip zip zap zap

12. The size of the new pizza amazed me; it was so big.

30-Second Timings

13. We all gazed upon the boxes of yellow raisins here.

14. Did the citizen act rudely at the bazaar yesterday?

15. Our feet were frozen and we felt like a big zombie.

1-Minute Timings

16. He sneezed when our team zoomed past the goal post.

17. We went on to victory: We learned our lessons well.

18. Zane was on the committee, but he hardly ever came.

15-Second Warm-ups (G, H, and I)

1. The good managers greeted the 45 guards with gusto.

2. Holly has to chop 36 bushes and 1 tree at her home.

3. In spite of ice, were those 14 or 15 bridges slick?

Learn the '7' Key   **Reach with the 'J' finger**

4. jjj 777 jjj 777 j7j j7j 7j7 7j7 jj7 jj7 77j 77j j7j

5. ju7 ju7 7uj 7uj u77 u77 77u 77u 77j 77j 7uj 7uj ju7

6. 75 java 771 joy 127 jiffy 775 jobs 616 juice 74 jut

Learn the '8' Key   **Reach with 'K' finger**

7. kkk 888 kkk 888 k8k k8k 8kk 8kk kk8 kk8 k8k k8k 88k

8. ki8 ki8 ii8 ii8 kk8 kk8 ki8 ki8 8ik 8ik i8k i8k ki8

9. 85 kite 885 kick 188 knot 288 know 388 kept 488 key

15-Second Warm-ups

1. Keith and Larry had a very quiet day away from all.

2. Jack and Jill went up the hill and tumbled down it.

3. The kittens went crazy when the small dogs arrived.

Learn the Hyphen Key   **Reach with the ';' finger**

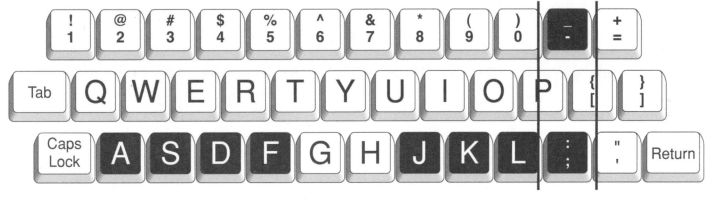

4. jjj j-j kkk k-k lll l-l ;;; ;-; j-- k-- l-- ;-- -j-

5. One-third of the ice-cream was one-sixth eaten now.

The dash is typed with two hyphens. Do not leave any space before or after the dash.

6. He said--again--that he was not going to Nashville.

Learn the Apostrophe Key   **Reach with ';' finger**

7. ''' ;;; ''' ;;; ';' ';' ;'; ;'; ''' ;;; ;'; ;'; '';

8. don't don't wouldn't wouldn't couldn't couldn't '';

9. Joe said he couldn't and wouldn't be here tomorrow.

18.   Gautama Buddha lived in northeast India about
       the 6th century B.C. He became the founder of the
       religion called Buddhism. Although he was of noble
       birth, Buddha was not proud and fond of luxury.
       Even when young, he was a serious and deep thinker.
       He decided it was better to lead a humble and
       religious life.

       When he was in his late twenties, he left his
       home and became a monk. He found strength in quiet
       meditation. He saw that the world was full of
       suffering, and he wanted to help people. So, he
       became a wandering teacher.

       Buddha said, first of all, that the worldly
       life cannot give final happiness. You should not be
       either overly indulgent or too strict with
       yourself. You should try to follow a middle path,
       keeping inner peace and discipline. The final state
       for a Buddhist is Nirvana, in which he is
       completely calm and free from any pain or anxiety.
       Buddha died when he was eighty years old. The main
       countries where Buddhism is practiced are Burma,
       Thailand, Ceylon, and Japan.

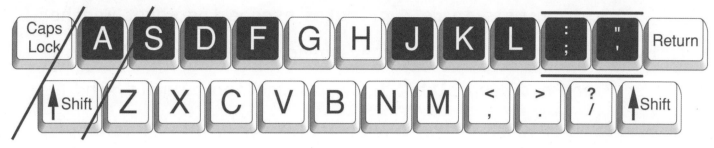

10. ;;; """ ;;; """ ;"; ;"; ""; ""; ;;" ;;" ";" ";" ;;"

11. Fred said, "I am going to buy an expensive washer."

12. "I don't know," said Gerry. She stayed in the jeep.

30-Second Timings

13. He said, "It's not my job to cover the telephones."

14. "I am not going," were her exact words to her sons.

15. "I don't have time." "She won't help me finish it."

1-Minute Timings

16. "I didn't do it and I don't know who ate the dips."

17. She said, "I have to take a long test on Thursday."

18. He was crazy to unload the machines before evening.

17.   Some animals in cold climates escape the worst weather

by hibernating. That is, they spend the winter months in a

very long and deep sleep. Many hibernating animals find

sheltered places underground, in caves, or at the base of

trees and hedges. Hibernating animals include bears, frogs,

lizards, bats, snails, tortoises, hedgehogs, and squirrels.

        During hibernation, the animal appears to be lifeless.

Breathing almost stops and the heartbeat is slow. The

animals are nourished by sugars stored in the liver and by

fat that has been built up during the summer. Some have been

known to return to the same place year after year to sleep.

Just as animals in cold climates escape winter by

hibernating, some in the tropics avoid hot, dry spells by

sleeping underground. This is known as aestivation, from the

Latin word meaning heat.

1. How many times do you space after a comma?

2. How many times do you space after a colon?

3. How many times do you space after a question mark?

4. How many times do you space after a semicolon?

5. Periods are placed (outside/inside) quotation marks?

6. Commas are placed (outside/inside) quotation marks?

7. The dash is typed with how many hyphens?

8. How many spaces do you leave before and after the dash?

9. How many spaces do you leave before or after a hyphen?

10. How many times do you space after a period at the end of a sentence?

11. Is the TAB key a toggle key?

12. Is the CAPS LOCK key a toggle key?

13. Which shift key would you press to type a 'C'?

14. Which shift key would you use to type an 'L'?

15. Which shift key would you use to type an 'M'?

16. Which shift key would you use to type an 'S'?

17. Which shift key would you press to make an 'H'?

18. Which shift key would you press to make a 'W'?

19. How many times do you space after a period used in an abbreviation such as Mr. or Mrs.?

Learn the '6' Key   Reach with 'J' finger

10. jjj 666 jjj 666 j6j j6j jj6 jj6 66j 66j j6j j6j j66

11. j66 j66 y66 y66 66y 66y 66j 66j y6y y6y yy6 yy6 jj6

12. 65 jugs 655 jacks 566 jury 166 jinks 616 jar 56 jug

30-Second Timings

13. The planes leave from gate 6 and 26 tomorrow night.

14. Fans in rows 3, 1, and 56 were unruly at the games.

15. The elevator host stopped at floors 2 and 4 and 16.

1-Minute Timing   S.I.—1.5

16.   Mercenaries are soldiers who give their services, and their lives if necessary, to anyone who will pay them enough money to do so. They were common even in ancient times. There are still men today whose love of adventure and action leads them to enlist with any army who will pay them enough.

SECTION C

Achieving Mastery

15-Second Warm-ups (D, E, and F)

1. Denni daydreamed of adding dozens of dollars daily.

2. Eli took 31 coffee breaks in 12 days of the events.

3. Fred fixed 23 mufflers but was fearful he forgot 2.

Learn the '4' Key　　　　　　**Reach with the 'F' finger**

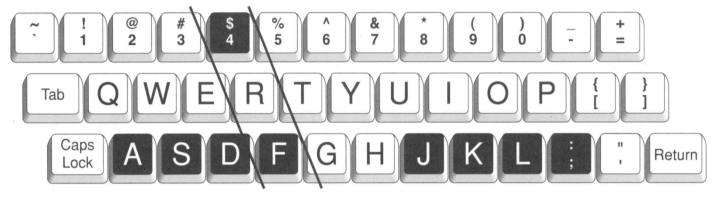

4. fff 444 fff 444 4f4 4f4 ff4 ff4 44f 44f fff 444 f4f

5. fr4 fr4 4rf 4rf r4r r4r 4r4 4r4 4rf 4rf fr4 fr4 4r4

6. 44 flew 43 fried 41 files 42 offer 14 foods 24 fled

Learn the '5' Key　　　　　　**Reach with 'F' finger**

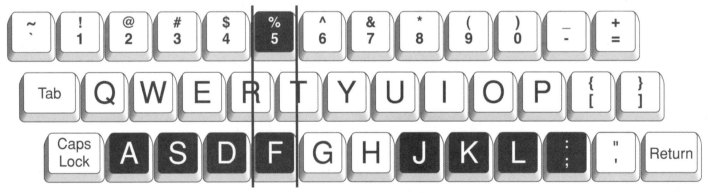

7. fff 555 fff 555 f5f f5f ff5 ff5 5f5 5f5 55f 55f f55

8. fr5 fr5 r55 r55 r5r r5r 55r 55r 55f 55f 5r5 5r5 5ff

9. 54 flax 515 fell 531 fluff 55 cuffs 15 farm 25 firm

Achieving Mastery on A-Words

15-Second Warm-ups

1. also arena attain area active about arbor acted art

2. awarded aqua atlas Alma apple awaited average actor

3. actual almost annual ace away airmail appeal arrays

4. aggravate adaptable paragraphs animals alfalfa gala

30-Second Timings

5. Alma ate an apple and pear salad while he was away.

6. Meanwhile, she appeared in an aqua dress at school.

7. The camping gear wasn't awarded at the town bazaar.

Make a 5-Space Paragraph Indentation at the beginning of a paragraph. To make a five-space paragraph indention place your hands on the home row and watch your left hand as the 'F' finger stays on the home row as a guide and the 'A' finger reaches up to press the TAB key. Do not space over five spaces instead of using the TAB key—it will show as an error.

Without actually pressing the tab key, practice the reach. Can you do it quickly without looking at the keys? Can you do it and leave the 'F' finger on the home row?

Word Wrap is the term used for the automatic flowing of words from one line to the next, without having to press the ENTER key each time as you have been doing. Word wrap is used when typing paragraphs. The only time you need to use the ENTER key is when you reach the end of the paragraph and need to begin a new paragraph.

18.   Animals are said to be mutants when they show characteristics different from the rest of their species. Mutations are processes by which the heredity properties of some of the cells in animals are altered. In nature these changes usually take place by chance and cannot be predicted. They are rare and little is known about the cause.

Today, the most common causes of mutations in animals are chemical substances and radiation. Radiation is rapidly becoming an increasing hazard.

Animals born from parents who have suffered the effects of more than normal radiation are almost always mutants. Cows have been known to grow a fifth leg. In the Pacific Islands, where nuclear tests have been conducted, there are fish which appear to have forgotten how to swim. They become disoriented and frequently beach themselves on the shore. Birds have lost the power to fly, and some may have only one wing.

Double Space (Leave One Blank Line) Between Paragraphs.

All the paragraph timings in Keyboard Mastery should be treated as single spaced paragraphs (meaning you should double space between paragraphs). The paragraph lines in the textbook are spaced to make them easier to read and easier to stay on the right line.

If you type fast enough, you might finish the paragraph before the timer stops you. Press the ENTER key twice (to double space between paragraphs), press the TAB key, and begin the paragraph again. Two paragraphs, with a double space between them would look like this:

(TAB) Lora was awarded an aqua atlas at the town bazaar. Alma was awarded some camping gear. Alan waited at home for an airmail letter from his aunt, which finally did arrive. (ENTER)
(ENTER)

(TAB) Lora was awarded an aqua atlas at the town bazaar. Alma was awarded some camping gear. Alan waited at home for an airmail letter from his aunt, which finally did arrive.

Technique Review

1. When typing paragraphs, the lines word wrap; you do not need to press the ENTER key after each line.

2. Pressing the ENTER key twice leaves one blank line between lines of type.

3. At the end of a paragraph, press the ENTER key twice (double space) and then press the TAB key to begin another paragraph.

1-Minute Timings   **S.I.—1.5**

8.   Lora was awarded an aqua atlas at the town bazaar. Alma was awarded some camping gear. Alan waited at home for an airmail letter from his aunt, which finally did arrive.

17.   Groups of elephants have been found buried
together both in Africa and Asia. The discovery of
a solitary elephant is rare. On the other hand, a
body in elephant country would usually soon
disappear owing to the activities of natural
scavengers.

Many people will argue that old elephants, when
their end is near, go to a legendary graveyard.
When an elephant is dying, it is not uncommon for
members of the herd to gather around and try to
revive it. When all hope is lost, they encircle it
as if in mourning at a funeral.

Achieving Mastery on B-Words

15-Second Warm-ups

9. bomb barb blab bribe blubber ebbs blow badge babble

10. busboy bramble bulb blob bobbin bringing blows boys

11. balloons blushing bubble brook abbey blew blue buzz

12. bagged bobcats bribery brought probable bobbing bat

30-Second Timings

13. The baby boy babbled words as his brothers bragged.

14. Big Bart bagged the bubbles from the brook in back.

15. The blue ribbons and badges were bribery to Brenda.

1-Minute Timing   S.I.—1.3

(Remember, paragraphs word wrap. If you finish the timing once, double-space, indent, and begin again.

16.   The barber bragged about what a bright boy he
     was. The bright boy was given a balloon for being
     so quiet. He was bashful, but brought the balloon
     to his brother to take to the abbey.

2-Minute Timing   S.I.—1.4

17.   The freshman year at college is often a scary
     time. One of my friends just told me that he was
     very eager to leave home. He soon found, however,
     that washing his clothes, paying his bills, and
     waking up on time were major adjustments. Without
     his mother's daily calls, he slept through many of
     his classes. His roommates let him sleep to teach
     him a lesson. He finally adjusted and enjoyed his
     new-found freedom.

10. ddd 333 ddd 333 d3d d3d 3d3 3d3 ddd 333 3d3 3d3 d3d

11. de3 de3 3ed 3ed ee3 ee3 33e 33e 3ed 3ed de3 de3 e3e

12. dent 33 dash 312 drip 311 darn 131 drag 123 dine 33

30-Second Timings

13. Sandi purchased 11 boxes each of items 12, and 231.

14. Dan found coins from the years 213, 1212, and 1213.

15. During the 2nd century there were probably 13 wars.

1-Minute Timing   **S.I.—1.4**

16.   Some sharks may attack human beings if they are

    attracted by underwater noises, erratic swimming,

    the presence of a large number of bathers, or the

    glint of jewelry. But probably the greatest

    attraction to a shark is the presence of blood,

    such as from a speared fish or live bait. Sharks

    are most likely to attack during the daytime and

    fairly near the shore where the water is shallow.

Achieving Mastery on C-Words

15-Second Warm-ups

1. cocoa crack occur ocean checks civic crates cardiac

2. chance yucca cutback concur chicken classic icicles

3. colic electric council choice cocky cinched comical

4. succeed succinct corrected economic concert critics

30-Second Timings

5. Chad cashed checks at the Civic Plaza on Ocean Ave.

6. Will Carole take a chance and cut the cactus plant?

7. The electric coil in the car cracked and is broken.

1-Minute Timing   S.I.—1.5

8.   Chris carried six crates crammed full of corn

and carrots. She wanted to cook chicken, too, but

the electrical connection to her pressure cooker

wasn't working correctly. The concert seems a

better choice due to these circumstances.

Achieving Mastery on D-Words

15-Second Warm-ups

9. eddy faded dozen dialed divides index oddly ordered

10. under buddy added coded doomed doodle danced deduce

11. faded dyed odds udder disdain dwindle fiddler diced

12. addendum saddles defended addressed saddened desire

15-Second Warm-ups (A, B, and C)

1. Amy ate a banana and lasagna and salad at a bazaar.

2. Flabby baby rabbits nibbled cabbage in our gardens.

3. Critical economic concerns occupy our civic cycles.

Learn the '1' Key   **Reach with the 'A' finger**

4. aaa qqq 111 aaa qqq 111 aaa 111 aaa 111 aaa qqq 111

5. aq1 aq1 1qa 1qa q1q q1q aq1 aq1 1qa 1qa 1qq 1qq 1qa

6. 11 ails 111 army 11 also 111 aqua 11 able 111 about

Learn the '2' Key   **Reach with 'S' finger**

7. sss 222 sss 222 s2s s2s ss2 ss2 22s 22s s2s s2s 222

8. sw2 sw2 2ws 2ws w2w w2w sw2 sw2 2ws 2ws 2ww 2ww 2ws

9. 12 stop 21 sold 11 scar 22 star 21 sass 12 stare 11

30-Second Timings

13. Eddie decided to buy a dozen fiddles for the dance.

14. Don was saddened to see the faded saddles for sale.

15. An addendum to the doomed deal was added and coded.

1-Minute Timing   S.I.—1.4

16.   Dean and Don decided to bid on the diamond. A
document was deeded after the sale to the highest
bidder. Dean dreaded bidding against a dwindling
audience. Don had to bid or the deal was doomed.

2-Minute Timing   S.I.—1.4

17.   A real good goal is to maintain good health. As
the first step, one should not develop the habit of
smoking. There is no doubt today that smoking leads
to cancer.

        A second habit that will help you maintain your
good health is to exercise vigorously several times
a week. Exercise is not only good for the heart,
but it aids in keeping your weight under control.
Exercise and proper diet will help you feel great.

SECTION D

Numbers and Symbols

Achieving Mastery on E-Words

15-Second Warm-ups

1. jewel cents eerie fence ever else edges even easily

2. verse geese cheese event keyed eleven deeded decree

3. emerge fewest coffee nerve excel degree breeze eyes

4. exceeds esteemed elected expenses referees believed

30-Second Timings

5. He esteemed the referees whose nerves excelled his.

6. There was an eerie feeling that seven were elected.

7. Fewer than eleven jewels were believed to be saved.

1-Minute Timing   S.I.—1.3

8.   Eleanor greeted the three executives from Erie with coffee and cheese crackers. They all felt they needed to lower the green fees of the three golf courses. It was also decreed that there were too many trees on the east end of one course.

Achieving Mastery on F-Words

15-Second Warm-ups

9. after cuffs offers jiffy fifty bluff stuff fork off

10. afford alfalfa falsify affirms affix afford fortify

11. baffled muffins faithful offset afflict traffic foe

12. affirm shuffled foodstuffs fearful offices fulfills

18.   Rabbits became a menace in Australia because
they breed so quickly and eat almost any vegetable.
Three pairs of rabbits were introduced into the
country in the eighteenth century. They multiplied
so rapidly that, with the addition of others which
were brought over, they spread over most of the
continent and caused a tremendous amount of damage.

The female rabbit, or doe, produces four to
eight litters of five to eight young in a year. At
the age of six months they are able to breed. It is
reckoned that a pair of rabbits, given ideal
conditions, could in three years have over thirteen
million descendants.

Many costly attempts to control the rabbits
failed in Australia. By the middle of the twentieth
century, a virus disease was introduced which
destroyed eighty percent in three years. They still
continue, however, to be a problem.

13. Fay fixed stuff while the baffled chef found forks.

14. Offer your faithful office friend forty foodstuffs.

15. The friendly fox affirmed that the foe was the cat.

1-Minute Timing   S.I.—1.5

16.   Traffic offenses in Fairtown baffle the fearful
officials. It was affirmed that five baffled
farmers flooded the court with files. The gruff
attorneys fled the courtroom in a fitful huff.

2-Minute Timing   S.I.—1.4

17.   Where there's a will, you can be absolutely
certain that your property will be disposed of as
you would like and that your loved ones will be
provided for--should something happen to you. Where
there's not a will, there can be dire consequences.

     No matter what your marital or financial
status, consider what would happen if you die
without a will: The state will determine your
heirs; a probate court will name a guardian for
your minor children if your spouse is not living;
plus, your estate may be subjected to unnecessary
death taxes.

13. A zoologist at the zoo watched the buzzard zoom in.

14. A magazine advertised a dozen pizzas to dazzle you.

15. Liz is lazy but she zooms into action when puzzled.

1-Minute Timing   S.I.—1.5

16.   The zoo amazes zillions of visitors daily. The
dazzling display from zebras to lizards puzzles
many folks with crazy antics. The graceful gazelles
graze in the plaza. After a day at the zoo, be sure
to stop at the bazaar and try a pizza.

2-Minute Timing   S.I.—1.4

17.   The longest snake in the world can be seen in
your local zoos. The Python is found in the
tropics, in and around the Malay region. It can
sometimes reach as much as thirty feet long. It
kills its prey by coiling itself around the animal
and hugging it so that it cannot breathe. Then the
snake swallows the victim whole. The Python is
strong as an ox, but chooses smaller animals which
it can swallow easily. Most Pythons live in trees.

The largest American snake is the Anaconda,
which lives in the rivers and swamps of Brazil,
Peru, and the Guineas.

Achieving Mastery on G-Words

15-Second Warm-ups

1. gangs gage eggs agog again gorge doggy baggy gauges

2. agree games gives soggy giggle anger aging gag gate

3. pegged haggle garages garbage luggage giggle haggle

4. baggage geology jogging debugging gorge gargle guys

30-Second Timings

5. Greg gave the green luggage to the guy at gate one.

6. Gayle will debug the game disk in the garage again.

7. The girls giggle as they jog with the geology guys.

1-Minute Timing   S.I.—1.3

8.   Gail and George haggle over who is going to pick

   green grapes. Gail suggests taking eggnog along to

   give to all the picking gang. George gritted his

   teeth and said that eggnog made him gag. George said

   he is grateful for the eggnog offer, but no thanks.

Achieving Mastery on H-Words

15-Second Warm-ups

9. huge hung home high held half heavy shush honor had

10. harsh hitch heavy hunch hits phony while help which

11. hauled hutch hatchet hardy healthy shake height hat

12. eighth thought hitchhiker hash hikers hotshot harsh

Achieving Mastery on Y-Words

15-Second Warm-ups

1. yes hour yolk easy year yule have may joys may yell

2. buyers enjoy layers today youth yield nearly yellow

3. nylon vinyl yonder canyon slyly young pyramid hobby

4. daydream loyalty yearly quality uncanny enjoy yacht

30-Second Timings

5. The young daydream of the new yearly yule bicycles.

6. The styles of yellow nylon and ugly vinyl is flaky.

7. Yesterday, Cathy yearned for a yacht or motorcycle.

1-Minute Timing   **S.I.—1.8**

8.   A hobby is healthy for anyone. It releases the
    symptoms of anxiety. You may enjoy flying or filling
    your days with tunes on a piano keyboard. Geology is
    an enjoyable hobby. Analyze your talents and try
    entirely new ways of releasing your creativity.

Achieving Mastery on Z-Words

15-Second Warm-ups

9. lazy zest fizz zing zero zeal buzz zooms gazed czar

10. lazy dozen dizzy pizza puzzle wizard zoo graze zinc

11. zigzag sizzle drizzle zealous dazzled hazard zombie

12. magazine zoologist citizens amazement hazardous zip

13. The heavy hatchet hit the healthy huge tree nearby.

14. With honor he held his head high and hauled hikers.

15. The eighth hitchhiker had a hunch Hale was a phony.

1-Minute Timing   S.I.—1.3

16.   Those happy chaps want to hike home before harsh weather happens. In a warm house they want a happy meal of ham and eggs, or hotcakes. It is a healthy, hearty breakfast. The chef is happy when the hikers help him complete his chores.

2-Minute Timing   S.I.—1.4

17.   Make your home life happier by treating the people you love as you do your other friends. What that means: Be polite to them. Treat your family members with courtesy and respect no matter what your mood is.

        If you are a bachelor about to be married, keep this thought in mind: The day after the wedding, phone the parents of the bride and tell them how lovely the wedding and reception was. This can go a long way in forming good relations with your new family.

18.   A newly hatched crocodile is about eight inches
long and can be found on the mud near the edge of
waters like marshes, rivers, and lakes around the
tropical regions of the world.

     Crocodile eggs are about the size of goose eggs
and are laid down in the mud. The nest is covered by
vegetation which rots and supplements the warmth of
the sun. The batch is guarded by the female until the
eggs are about to hatch. Then the crocodile digs
down to free them from the mud.

     Adult crocodiles vary in size from about three
feet to almost twenty feet. Some are man-eaters and
will attack and eat almost any living creature that
comes within their reach. They were once thought to
weep as they snapped up their victim. That is why in
popular speech we often hear about the false display
of sorrow as crocodile tears.

Achieving Mastery on I-Words

15-Second Warm-ups

1. iris ideas ice skiing insist icily chili idle inked

2. idiom bike will bikini idiot sail skill trip infirm

3. inhibit impair impish digits hiring inflict idolize

4. limiting imitate militia abilities insulin inclined

30-Second Timings

5. Irene has ideas of baking chili on her skiing trip.

6. The biker is inclined to insist upon going sailing.

7. Imitating the abilities of the militia is limiting.

1-Minute Timing   **S.I.—1.6**

8.   Kim is inclined to inflict ire on civilians who insist on inviting the military outside the city limits of Miami. I imagine she will invite them home sometime for chili. If so, I think she will insist on obeying civil law.

Achieving Mastery on J-Words

15-Second Warm-ups

9. jabs jars joke jaws jerk joint jolly jams jump jail

10. major jelly jeers junk jumbo judge joint jeeps jade

11. joined janitor jealous juniors jaywalk juice jurors

12. javelin adjourned judicial juveniles adjusted judge

13. The exterior of the taxi was examined on a pretest.

14. The experts who examined it excluded exotic extras.

15. The six boxes were an excellent hoax to expose him.

1-Minute Timing   S.I.—1.7

16.   If you would only examine the exhaust pipe on the taxi, you could fix it before the exterior was exposed to cracking. The extra test on the taxi is a luxury and is expensive. The exasperated executives exploded at the extra costs involved.

2-Minute Timing   S.I.—1.3

17.   Nearly all birds use their wings for flight, but penguins use theirs as paddles for swimming. They spend most of their lives in the sea and find their food there. Although many birds can both swim and fly, no other bird can swim as well as the flightless penguins.

     Penguins have muscles, bones, and organs very much like those of flying birds. At one time they may have been able to fly. However, twenty-five million years ago fossils show that there were penguins very much like those alive today.

13. The judge adjusted the judicial system for juniors.

14. Jason was jealous of the janitor and jeered at him.

15. An injured jaywalker justified himself to the jury.

1-Minute Timing   S.I.—1.2

16.   Jim enjoyed the jumbo jars of juicy jams and

    jellies. To get more jam, he mixed a jug of juice

    with the jelly and poured it into jam jars. The

    lids on the jars of jelly and jam just got mixed. Oh

    well, jam or jelly is just fine for Jim.

2-Minute Timing   S.I.—1.4

17.   Would you like some tips on taking care of your

    dog or cat? Garlic has natural flea-repelling

    agents and is a natural antibiotic. To add garlic

    to the diet of your pet, marinate a fourth clove of

    crushed garlic into an eighth teaspoon of tamari

    sauce and mix it into your cat's food.

    Table scraps are rarely good for your pets. In

    fact, chocolate and cocoa are poisonous for both

    cats and dogs. Never give your pets any food

    containing any amount of these ingredients.

Achieving Mastery on W-Words

15-Second Warm-ups

1. who when want wake week win with wise were bow well

2. award wafer waves widow wonder swarm power scowl we

3. wrist frown swallow water welfare wages reward yawn

4. waterway windowsill worthwhile crawled prowler wire

30-Second Timings

5. The swift cowboy will win the gold crown this week.

6. Waterways make power worthwhile for use, not waste.

7. The weak dog howled and growled at the wet prowler.

1-Minute Timing   S.I.—1.3

8.   The newscast might show a winning war. The
newsman can draw a wide range of viewers, which is
his reward for daily news well written. Adding wit
and wisdom to a newscast will reward the newscaster
with good reviews. Witless words can wreck a well-
planned newscast.

Achieving Mastery on X-Words

15-Second Warm-ups

9. oxen minx hoax axis exam text exit taxi box fix six

10. extras expert expects examine excess reflex extreme

11. relax mixing mystic luxury exciting exotic excluded

12. exterior excellent pretext mixture saxophone excuse

Achieving Mastery on K-Words

15-Second Warm-ups

1. kink kitty kinky kinds kettle kick kilts picks knee

2. kayaks knack knock kings track skunk knotty kinfolk

3. knolls kinship skylark baking knuckle makes tankers

4. kickback knockout fickle kennels bookkeeper skilled

30-Second Timings

5. The keen kennel keeper kicked his skinny knee hard.

6. Keri is a bookkeeper that keeps kayaks in the lake.

7. The skipper wore kilts as he baked in the kitchens.

1-Minute Timing   S.I.—1.2

8.   Kamas had his skull kicked when he tackled the king's men for a knockout. His weakness was in his knees. The fickle king was skilled in keeping track of the knockouts. His knack was to ask for a kickback in kayaks.

Achieving Mastery on L-Words

15-Second Warm-ups

9. lads lull fall skill allow alone flute locks elope

10. ladle libel ankle frills below legally shall level

11. fellow lately locally gallery parallel likable lot

12. volleyball hillbilly liberal fulfill willfully Lon

18.   The Abominable Snowman, or Yeti, is half human

and half ape according to the legend among the

Nepalese of the high Himalayas. Nepalese mothers use

the tradition of the Yeti to scare their disobedient

children, telling them that the Yeti will get them

if they don't watch out. It is a popular warning.

        No one can say whether or not the Yeti actually

exists. The first apparent confirmation of its

existence came with photographs of huge footprints

in the snow taken by a mountaineer. Only a few

people claim to have seen the Yeti and some believe

it to be invisible.

        Skins which the Nepalese say have been taken

from dead Yetis turn out to be those of either the

Serow Goat-antelope or the rare Tibetan blue bear.

Tracks in the snow said to be the footprints of the

Yeti have proven to be those of a snow leopard, a

bear, a wolf, or a fox, which have melted to form

the larger, human-like tracks of the Yeti.

Nevertheless, the legend lingers and it may yet be

proven to have a basis in fact.

13. A local fellow was playing volleyball on the floor.

14. The fall made her legally liable and she shall pay.

15. Larry is a loyal lad with liberal leanings in love.

1-Minute Timing   S.I.—1.3

16.   Lilly loves frills on her collars, like lace.
       She willfully paid eleven dollars for the lapel on
       her coat. A fellow billed her for a lily she lost at
       the polls. It fell on the floor and was finally
       located. She will not lose the lily again.

2-Minute Timing   S.I.—1.4

17.   For better time management, never lose your
       train of thought. If you have to leave a job in the
       middle, at least finish the task at hand--write
       that sentence, add up that column of figures, make
       that last phone call. Then write yourself a note on
       how you plan to finish the project.

           The difference between being a manager and
       being a leader is largely a matter of approach.
       Managers cope with solving complex problems.
       Leaders cope with change, and trying to motivate
       others in the right direction.

30-Second Timings

13. Elvis invited the visitors to see his silver vests.

14. Camping is a valid vacation for a savvy individual.

15. Veal served with clove spice makes a savory flavor.

1-Minute Timing   S.I.—1.7

16.   A visit to a very old village gives vim and vigor to the adventurer. Heavy problems vanish and nerves revive; a valuable and worthwhile endeavor. A visit to a volcano serves to appreciate past events. Take advantage of events that elevate the mind.

2-Minute Timing   S.I.—1.5

17.   The eggs of frogs become tadpoles within two weeks of being laid in the water. Tadpoles may take anywhere from two months to three years to change completely into frogs. The time taken seems to depend upon their environment. Tadpoles will usually develop faster in warmer waters.

          Tadpoles, like fish, breathe through gills. They develop lungs during the changeover, gain legs and lose their tails. Their menu also changes from plants to very small insects.

Achieving Mastery on M-Words

15-Second Warm-ups

1. meal made mine memo move motor memo mama move makes

2. amends making melons armory munch immune tombs must

3. memory humming summary merger remnants mess mammoth

4. momentum maximum amendment amused rambling hamsters

30-Second Timings

5. The meals of melon and omelets made many feel warm.

6. Many rambling hamsters were climbing on the motors.

7. Maria's memory of guns humming led to an amendment.

1-Minute Timing   S.I.—1.4

8.   The merger of a monthly academy on campus may take

place in autumn. It may bring mixed emotions from

both men and women. Many think the merger will amount

to more time, expense, and mass meetings. Let them

make amends and make the academy some other time.

Achieving Mastery on N-Words

15-Second Warm-ups

9. Nancy nail nice pink banjo nouns inns noon none not

10. nanny cannon ransom nurse handle singer fence annoy

11. known cannot dinner notation scanner insane banning

12. inventors convicts nightly swinging unknown annoyed

Achieving Mastery on U-Words

15-Second Warm-ups

1. urge upon up undo unit urge user luau jute uses pup

2. unite usury unduly useful furry fruit humans judges

3. until usual unsure public lucky unruly uranium duty

4. unusually curriculum unglued untruthful utilize urn

30-Second Timings

5. I am unsure if the user uses uranium to utilize it.

6. It is untruthful to urge anyone to buy junky autos.

7. The number was unusually lucky--until luck ran out.

1-Minute Timing   S.I.—1.5

8.   Biscuits and fruit juices are used for lunch or

brunch. An unusual form of lunch or dinner is the

luau. The luau should be included in any curriculum

unit on foreign cooking. Cucumbers and squash can be

added for a unique and useful side dish.

Achieving Mastery on V-Words

15-Second Warm-ups

9. ever vase very vast vows move vines vests evil veal

10. valid invite silver heavy clever savvy savory vivid

11. evolved velvet village rivals elevate vanish events

12. valuable endeavor revolved volcano vacation invited

30-Second Timings

13. A nurse named Nancy cannot handle the dinner notes.

14. The insane convict was swinging a blue ransom note.

15. Norma will make pink banjos and mingle with diners.

1-Minute Timing   **S.I.—1.4**

16.   The banker insisted that none of the new notes needed to come in. It was unknown how many notes were nixed by the scanner. The manager said to announce to every agent that he/she should insert new names in the notes.

2-Minute Timing   **S.I.—1.4**

17.   Some bad deals never get better. Credit life insurance is a case in point. It pays off the balance of the loan to the lender if the borrower dies. Consumers usually pay too much for credit life, and few people need it in the first place.

    One reason for the high cost has to do with the way credit life is sold. Lenders offer borrowers just one policy; the consumer can't shop around. To earn the highest possible commission on their credit insurance sales, lenders tend to affiliate with the insurer whose rates are highest.

18.   We all know that birds build nests. Some find

trees the most convenient. Others prefer hedges,

the eaves of roofs, chimney pots, rocky ledges or

holes in trees. But, what does a bird do that can

neither fly nor swim?

        Living on the dry, open plains of eastern and

southern Africa, the ostrich takes no pains to hide

its nest. It merely finds a shallow depression in

the ground and scoops out some more dirt if

necessary. The hole may be up to three yards

across. In it are laid six to eight eggs, each one

by a different female. Then one hen and one cock

take turns guarding the two and a half pound eggs

until they are ready to hatch.

        However, the ostrich does not sit on its eggs to

incubate them. It squats between them spreading its

wings to provide shade and keep them from cooking

in the hot desert sun.

Achieving Mastery on O-Words

15-Second Warm-ups

1. odor oboe book loop door roof robot stool cool zone

2. voodoo oblong outgo option organ ornate snoop prose

3. somehow troops points office often cocoons offshoot

4. onlooker schoolroom drooped footstool boring olives

30-Second Timings

5. A snoopy shopper bought a stool for the schoolroom.

6. The prowler somehow opened the doors to the office.

7. Omar chose a most boring poem from a book of prose.

1-Minute Timing   S.I.—1.3

8.   The bookstore was outdoors on the rooftop and

looked out over a lot of old shops. The store was

full of shoppers and onlookers. The textbooks and

workbooks were poised on a broken bookcase. I hope

it doesn't snow.

Achieving Mastery on P-Words

15-Second Warm-ups

9. pups prop port plant play prep pipe pave plot ponds

10. poise places maple plans pears pumped report peered

11. report pompous popping promptly floppy pamper party

12. puppeteer pleasant duplicate platform purpose pulse

---

13. The tall, thin tutor tried to tell two witty tales.

14. Tim traded the gentle cattle for a native tortoise.

15. The writer throws a tantrum if the text is trimmed.

1-Minute Timing   S.I.—1.5

16.   It is necessary to be quiet when taking a test
in a class. The time to talk is when the teacher
asks the students questions. Then, be sure to
answer courteously and politely. Always be prepared
by reading the textbook and doing the assignments.

2-Minute Timing   S.I.—1.4

17.   Vampire bats are dangerous because they carry
rabies and other diseases. They infect their
victims as they suck the blood, which is their only
food.

     Vampire bats are found only in South and
Central America. They have extremely sharp teeth
and pierce the skin of their prey so gently that
the victim does not awaken. Blood is drawn into the
mouth by the almost tubular tongue. The digestive
system of the vampire bat is specially adapted for
his diet of blood.

13. Pattie planted a pretty maple tree on the platform.

14. The report plans pompous support for a spring prom.

15. Pat peeled the ripe pears while the popcorn popped.

1-Minute Timing   S.I.—1.5

16.   Perhaps the purpose of pampering puppies is to
promote a pleasant disposition. Dogs are playful
and like to be petted, especially if you have
pampered them as puppies. Being kind to animals
will pave the way for real friendships.

2-Minute Timing   S.I.—1.4

17.   Soap and detergent can dry the skin because
they remove its natural oils. Once its oil coating
is gone, the skin gives up water readily and
becomes dry and flaky. Many young people can suffer
from dry skin, especially in winter when humidity
outdoors is low and central heating makes the
indoors dry as a desert.

          Most soaps have emollients, which may help seal
in moisture. If you have dry skin, however, don't
look to some magic soap formula for relief. Apply
baby oil or a moisturizing cream after bathing
while the skin is still damp.

Achieving Mastery on S-Words

15-Second Warm-ups

1. sash skis soars sand sees boss sets roses says zest

2. Susan sudsy sense stress trust sissy sassy asset is

3. masses assists seasons disks hostess unsure success

4. obsesses scissors assassins glasses dresses assigns

30-Second Timings

5. Susan washes her dresses as she assists her sister.

6. The hostess set roses on the table to stress smell.

7. Sally was unsure of her success with sewing sashes.

1-Minute Timing   S.I.—1.3

8.   Our boss says he may speak to the issue of stress

and trust in the summer meeting. As gifts, he may

give all his employees six quarts of berries. He is

obsessed with solving several problems in our jobs.

He wants to be sure his employees are successful.

Achieving Mastery on T-Words

15-Second Warm-ups

9. tall thin tells team text tart try tutor time tried

10. trades store cattle typed witty tattle tastes truth

11. writes attest attract typical gentle acting treason

12. testing tantrum tortoise trimming astute native Tim

Achieving Mastery on Q-Words

15-Second Warm-ups

1. quits quick quote quad quiz queen aqua quiet acquit

2. squad quite quire inquire quarts square equip quota

3. qualify quantity liquid unique request quizzed quid

4. quarterly quicksand quotient questions requirements

30-Second Timings

5. The queen questioned the quality of an antique jar.

6. The quotients on the quarterly quiz met the quotas.

7. Our squads quickly acquired the liquid for quinine.

1-Minute Timing   S.I.—1.4

8.   At the request of a unique friend, the drill
   squad questioned and quizzed the quintet about the
   quicksand. Will it qualify and meet requirements of
   quick action? The thought of the quarterly quota is
   enough to make one quake.

Achieving Mastery on R-Words

15-Second Warm-ups

9. raves lark near rear rare rain roar purr dare rerun

10. urban heard words large reef worry hurry sorry tart

11. rumors arrears warrant restore warden rupture angry

12. eardrum barrier overrun dirty reporter rancher hash

30-Second Timings

13. The rumors were a barrier to good reporting by Rex.

14. An eardrum that is ready to rupture should be rare.

15. Rent that is in arrears will warrant harsh reports.

1-Minute Timing   S.I.—1.3

16.   In poorer countries there is little to purchase goods and services with. The grim truth is that salaries are small and products are rare. The rows and rows of produce and other products have prices that are out of reach to these consumers.

2-Minute Timing   S.I.—1.3

17.   For much of the world, cereal grains supply the main source of dietary protein. Meat comes with too high a price in developing countries. Beef is a highly consumed meat in the United States, averaging sixty-seven pounds per person each year.

     Beef production requires a lot of natural resources: grain, the land the grain grows on, and water. It takes six to eight pounds of grain to produce a pound of beef, compared with about four pounds of grain to produce a pound of pork, and two pounds to produce a pound of chicken.